Joseph Heckelman

THE FIRST JEWS IN THE NEW WORLD

THE DRAMATIC ODYSSEY OF THE EARLY JEWS INTO THE WESTERN HEMISPHERE

JOSEPH HECKELMAN

Jay Street Publishers New York, NY 10023

Cover Illustration:
Portion of Americae Sive Novi Orbis
Antwerp 1592 (Originally published in 1587)
Courtesy The Colonial Williamsburg Foundation, Williamsburg, VA.

First Printing – 2004
Second Printing – 2005
Third Printing – 2007
Fourth Printing – 2013

ISBN 1-889534-94-3

Published by Jay Street Publishers, New York, NY 10023

To my wife, Elaine,
and to Jay, Leah, Kevin
and our grandchildren

I wish to thank Harold Jacobs for his continuing encouragement in the drafting of this book. In addition, I am indebted to Rabbis Anthony D. Holz, William Rosenthall and David Radinsky for their reading and comments on the early drafts. I would like to thank Walter H. Weiner for his efforts regarding this project. And my sincere appreciation to my wife, Elaine, for her support during the many long months spent in writing this book.

TABLE OF CONTENTS

FOREWARD

By Rabbi Dr. Marc D. Angel, Senior Rabbi of Congregation Shearith Israel in New York (founded 1654); author of "Remnant of Israel: A Portrait of America's First Jewish Congregation – Shearith Israel" (Riverside Book Company, 2004).

The "New World" was a mysterious and promising domain to the European kingdoms of the 16th and 17th centuries. Explorers and settlers crossed the ocean in search of gold and spices, new realms of wealth and power. Christian missionaries came to convert the natives and impose their religious world view on them. With the Europeanization of the Americas world history took a dramatic turn.

Amid the small but growing number of European newcomers to this part of the world were people of Jewish extraction, as well as practicing Jews. Conversos came to the New World hoping to leave the Inquisitions of Spain and Portugal behind them and perhaps even to return to open Jewish life. Sadly the Inquisitions followed them to the New World. Ex-conversos, many of whom had come back to Judaism in Amsterdam and other West European centers, came to the Americas as merchants and adventurers – and they laid the foundations for Jewish life in the New World.

The story of these early Jewish settlements is fascinating, even inspiring. Though few in number, the Jewish colonists established vibrant congregations and maintained their religious traditions. With the establishment of Shearith Israel in New Amsterdam in 1654, the North American Jewish community was launched. Shearith Israel was the lone Jewish congregation in North America for nearly eighty years, and the only Jewish congregation in New York City until 1825. The colonial American Jewish congregations in New York, Newport, Philadelphia,

Savannah and Charleston were the pioneer congregations of American Jewry. They fought for, and won, the basic rights which we all enjoy today. They participated actively in the establishment of the United States, serving the American cause through their support of and participation in the American Revolution.

Joseph Heckelman is to be thanked for writing this book to tell the story of the early Jewish communities in the New World. In spite of the considerable scholarly research about them, the general public is remarkably unaware of the contributions and sacrifices of the early generations of American Jews. Yet, those Jewish men and women who came to the Americas in the 16th – 18th centuries were genuine pioneers. They brought Judaism to these shores and they participated significantly in the development of the New World.

One of the distinctive qualities of the Jewish people is our collective memory. We remember all our generations and feel organically linked to them. This book will help deepen our connection with and appreciation of the early Jewish settlers of the New World – our spiritual forebears.

INTRODUCTION

The Journey of the First Jews to the American Colonies

The many events going on in the world in the 14th, 15th and 16th centuries, particularly the Spanish and Portuguese Inquisitions, set the stage for the initial Jewish travels to the Western Hemisphere. Through innumerable twists and turns major Jewish communities were established on the east coast: Shearith Israel in New York, Mickve Israel in Savannah, the Touro Synagogue in Newport, Rhode Island, Mikveh Israel in Philadelphia and Kahal Kadosh Beth Elohim in Charleston, South Carolina.

This book will recount the historic events leading to the formation of the earliest congregations and synagogues on the east coast of the United States. It will cover the periods from the expulsions of the Jews from Spain and Portugal; the initiation of the Jewish communities in Amsterdam and London; the settlement of Jews in Brazil in the 16th century through the mid-17th century; the major movement to the islands of the Caribbean, and the arrival of the first Jewish immigrants to the east coast colonies. The early history of the five key settlement cities that Jews occupied in the colonial period will be told, as well as the events surrounding the establishment of the early congregations.

It's a story far different from that of the later Jews entering through Castle Garden, and then Ellis Island. Most people are familiar with the predominantly Ashkenazi movement (Jews from Central and Eastern Europe) into the United States starting in the 1820s, and with vastly increased numbers coming as the "huddled masses" from the 1870s through the early 1900s.

This book deals with a much earlier period. The first

Jews to the Western Hemisphere followed an entirely different path, eventually resulting in the first congregations and synagogues in Brazil, the Caribbean and the American colonies.

There were no welcoming reception centers such as Ellis Island. Rather, Jews traveled under great hardships to the wilderness of South America and entered Mexico at the time of Hernando Cortez. They faced the Spanish and Portuguese Inquisitions in the New World, and fought for religious equality and civic tolerance. The Jews immigrated in small numbers, and were a religious minority that, for the most part, were not only not welcomed, but were hounded for their religious beliefs. Their tenacity in establishing their communities in the Western Hemisphere, and in defending their civic and religious rights, is little short of amazing. These early Jewish settlers led the way to the eventual establishment of some five and one-half to six million Jews in the United States.

To relate this odyssey, we need to look back many centuries, to the appalling world of riots against the Jews, the Inquisition and the expulsion of the Jews from the Iberian Peninsula in the late 15th century. It is a world of age-old religious hatreds that created New Christians, Marranos and crypto-Jews, but also an age of worldwide exploration by Spain, Portugal and the Dutch in the 15th through 17th centuries.

1

MUSLIM CONTROL OF SPAIN AND THE *RECONQUISTA*

Jews had been in Spain and Portugal from at least the 2nd century. A number of Germanic tribes (including the Vandals) had entered Spain starting in the 5th Century, and by about 600 CE Christian Visigoths had assumed control by vanquishing the other tribes. The Visigoths then would turn their attention to the persecution of the most visible minority in their kingdom – the Jews. Edicts required baptism or death, and, unfortunately, thousands of Jews were impacted. There were concerns regarding expulsions or even enslavement.

In the 7th and 8th centuries Muslims swept across the Middle East and North Africa, and Moors (nomadic people of North Africa, mainly Berbers and Arabs) entered Spain in 711, led by the Berber Tarik ibn Ziyad. The Visigoth Kingdom was ended.

The place of the crossing to Spain was named 'Jabel-al-Tarik' (or Tarik's Mountain) after their leader. This name has been corrupted over time into Gibralter. The Muslims continued their planned conquest of Europe by pouring over the Pyrenees Mountains into France, but were stopped by Charles Martell (the grandfather of Charlemagne) in the Battle of Tours in 732-733.

In 756 a Muslim dynasty was established in Córdoba, with the area growing in wealth, architectural beauty and culture. Toledo, Córdoba and Seville grew into centers of learning, with great universities and architecture renowned to this day. Skilled artisans in various media such as wood, leather, textiles and plasterwork came from Morocco and other Muslim areas, and outstanding mosques and palatial buildings were being added to these cultural centers. It was a time as well for major intellectual scholarship and rich contributions by Muslims in fields such as art, architecture, science, medicine, language, letters, mathematics and the teaching and study of Greek philosophy.

Jews were able to advance both intellectually and economically under Moorish rule despite periods of persecution, and vicious campaigns by Berber tribes to convert Jews to Islam. These anti-Jewish activities increased in ferocity by the mid 1100s. Despite the attacks, Jewish cultural and religious activity flourished. And, considering what the future would hold, these were times of relative tolerance, allowing for a truly historic period of Jewish culture, religious activity and study of Jewish law.

This period saw development of schools of advanced Hebrew teaching in places like Granada, Seville, Barcelona, Lucena and Toledo; the writing of historically important rabbinic texts and commentaries, and the writing of glowing poetry by Samuel ha-Nagid, Moses ibn Ezra, Judah Halevi and Dunash ben Labrat. Rabbinic commentaries were being written in Barcelona, Seville, Grenada and Toledo. And the Jewish vizar, Hidai ibn Shaprut, in Córdoba, fostered advanced Hebrew literature in the 10th century under Caliph Abd al-Rahman III. But things were changing for the worse.

Maimonides (Moses ben Maimon), left Spain with his family in his teens due to growing Muslim fundamentalism, going to Fez, Acre and finally Cairo. This scholar and physician would later write the *Mishnah Torah*, a compilation of Jewish law, *Thirteen Principles of the Faith* and the *Guide to the Perplexed.* He discussed philosophic and religious questions concerning the existence of God, the principles of creation and addressed metaphysical as well as medical problems.

The political and religious issues then were complex and, in many ways, mirror our times. While a good portion of the country was under Muslim control, many Muslim and Jewish communities were under Christian rule. And when the Christians regained territory from the Moors, various Islamic groups would appear, mainly from Morocco, to defend Muslim areas and the Islamic religion. Then, as now, there were competing groups with various degrees of fundamentalism. The Almoravids, who maintained a rather rigid and severe form of Islam, were called in by the Moors in Spain to aid in stemming the tide of Christian reconquest. They would rule Muslim areas in the 11th and 12th centuries, and for good measure took control of the more moderate Muslims, governing areas of Muslim Spain and Northern Morocco. These rulers expressed contempt of the luxurious, elaborate Muslim life that had evolved.

In time the Christians, who retained the northern areas of Spain commenced a 'Reconquista', the recapture for Christendom. It did not happen in one grand sweep, but over time there was a gradual extinction of Muslim control. There was no true central governmental structure during Muslim rule, with the various geographic areas essentially defending themselves. A Christian curtain was falling from north to south from about 1050 to 1492. The Almoravids were, in turn, replaced by the even more fundamentalist Almohads, who would rule much of the Muslim controlled areas during the 12th and 13th centuries. The Almohads saw themselves as the true purifiers of Islam.

Muslim Spain was persecuting the Jewish minority. The Almohads destroyed the very active Jewish cultural life, and some Jews had to leave their homes and escape to the more northerly parts of Christian controlled Spanish areas that, at that time, were more benign. And the Almohads were one more group of people in a seemingly endless line who most assuredly knew what God wanted and were eager to harshly convert the untutored infidels. The Almohads rule lasted to about 1232.

Despite attempts to retain the land for Islam, the waves of Christian conquest saw the extent of Muslim control slowly shrink during the 11th to 13th centuries, with the Christians regaining Toledo in 1085, and the victory of Navas de Tolosa by the Spanish and Portuguese in 1212 initiated the final downfall of Moorish Spain. Fredrick III (1199-1252) captured Córdoba in 1236, and Seville and Valencia in 1248. There was now Christian domination from north to south, and by 1250 Granada in the south was the sole major surviving area under Muslim control.

Many in the Muslim and Jewish communities remained in Christian captured areas. It was a time of tentative, but hopeful 'convivencia' between Muslims, Christians and Jews in the northern part of the country – a time that allowed them, to a degree, – to live near one another, and to somewhat understand their neighbors' faith and customs. Despite the high sounding purposes of 'convivencia,' in practice, Jews and Muslims were just barely tolerated. While it was a time of some tolerance, the tolerance was under the very careful eyes of the governing Christians and the church. Muslim and Jewish religious services were allowed. But social and religious distinctions were always clearly apparent and always close to the surface. The use of Muslims or Jews to mind Christian children was forbidden; social and sexual activities with Christians were under heavy penalties including death, and in 1252, for example, Alfonso X decreed that Moors and Jews must kneel when a Christian priest carried the bread for the Eucharist in a public procession.

Mosques were also being converted to churches. To put some perspective on these restrictions, it should be remembered that Christians under earlier Islamic rule also were restricted from building churches, ringing church bells, and from holding religious processions.[1] A true 'convivencia' did not always work out in practice. However, many Muslims, known as Mudejars, would remain and continue their faith and their language for centuries.

The increasing waves of Christian religious zealotry and hatred destroyed this period of co-existence and intellectual flowering. Intense periods of persecution and murder would follow as Spanish Christians fervently undertook their Reconquista. The calls for Reconquista would be growing more insistent with time, and the church and the people were prepared to pick up knives and torches. The Reconquista would turn into both a religious-based war against the 'infidels' and 'heretics' in their midst, and as well, a means to acquire land and wealth for the aristocratic land owners and the church and its ruling class.

Heretics and dissidents from the Catholic Church were targeted, with an increasing number of violent and horrific acts directed against both Jews and Moors. For Jews these stated purposes led to forcible or voluntary conversions through baptism, the elimination of Judaic ritual observances, and in time, would lead to expulsion.[2] As Alexis de Tocqueville remarked regarding the French Revolution – he had almost always seen the spirit of religion and the spirit of freedom marching in opposite directions.

From the dark and cool cathedrals came a continual stream of vicious sermons that exacerbated issues and focused problems on whatever minorities suited their purposes and served to inflame listeners to action. As usual, Jews were then, as now, always in season, but they were not the only group being persecuted. Christian groups whose dogma did not coincide with Vatican dogma were also subject to violent actions by the Catholic Church. In the Middle Ages popes were highly concerned about the spread of various religions and philosophies that did not agree with Rome's dogmatic beliefs. The dogma of the Catholic Church was being questioned. Increasingly harsh instructions and methodology were being promulgated by Rome for dealing with 13th century European heretics. A papal driven assault in the early 1200s against these heretics would, in fact, establish the methods used in the Spanish Inquisition, some two and a half centuries later.

In 1208 Pope Innocent III was desirous of ending the fairly widespread religious belief of Catharism (known as well as Albigensianism) that was gaining adherents in southern France. The belief within Catharism, as denoted by Albert Shannon, was that there were two gods: the god in heaven who was spiritual and created all spiritual things, including man's soul, and the evil god that created all material things, including man but not his soul. And in another concept of Catharism there was a good god and an evil god (a god of light and a god of darkness), and they were in eternal opposition and conflict. By 1233 Pope Gregory IX promulgated instructions that would end what the church believed were heretic beliefs. The instructions laid out the process of witness accusations, interrogations, and the detailed recording by notaries of the inquisitorial process. This process was put under the control of Dominicans. The pope stated that he was opposed to "free-lance" killing of the heretics, and desired a more structured and controlled inquisition.

The Inquisitional process was being perfected that at a later time would be used against the Jews in Spain and Portugal. While torture was not initially practiced, Innocent IV (1243-1254) later did approve its use in cases of heresy. The inquisitional management process (and if you will, this developing working model), was slowly evolved during the 13th century, and was then used by Spain in an amazingly similar manner.

There was a direct correlation between the number of heretics burned and the amount of money and property flowing into the hands of the nobles during the 13th century Albigensian suppression. The capturing and naming of persons as heretics was proving to be very profitable. The extent and variety of the medieval inquisitions and Crusades from the 11th – 14th centuries on demonstrate that the Spanish and Portuguese Inquisitions and the methods to be used were, unfortunately, not an aberration in world history, but a part of a well trod path of man's inhumanity to man. And it is thought that an instruction to crusaders in 13th century France in burning people alive (and in most cases not even knowing who, if anyone, was "guilty"), was "Kill all, kill all, for God will know his own."[3]

14th, 15th CENTURY ANTI-JEWISH RIOTS

Hatred towards Jews grew in intensity in the 1200s in Castile, Aragon and Catalonia. There were campaigns to have Jews renounce their faith, either voluntarily or forcefully. The growth of anti-Semitism, fomented in large part by the Dominican order, finally exploded throughout Spain, and any attempts to calm the population were overwhelmed by the inflammatory atmosphere of hatred, abetted by weekly Roman Catholic sermons.

By the mid-13th century there were movements among the Christians to "purify" Spanish Catholicism. Economic catastrophes (as well as the bubonic plagues) in the late 1340s set in motion virulent anti-semitism that increased in intensity over the coming decades, aided by a consistent torrent of hatred emanating from the pulpit. Jews were generally city dwellers, and that made them conveniently accessible to the mobs.

During the long centuries when Jews and Muslims were welcomed in Spain, Jews were involved in normal commerce and trade, and were found in roles close to the seat of power, particularly as related to finance, taxes and governmental policy, and money lending – activities that were certain to incite resentment and hostility. In some local areas Jews were given political power over the Muslims. There generally were restrictions that did not allow Christians to be involved in the money lending trade, and some Jews found that activity to be their only option in earning a living.

In particular, the population was incited to violence by Ferrant Martinez, a fanatical deacon, who used to openly state, "Kill all who refuse baptism." In 1378 he proposed to settle the "Jewish problem" by destroying all 23 synagogues in Seville, confining all Jews to restricted areas, stopping all contact with them and removing them from positions of influence. Walled city enclosures for Jews, with controlled access points, were used in Spain and Portugal in the 14th century. The term "ghetto" was first used in Venice in 1516, when the area of enclosure for Jews was a foundry, or "ghetto" in Italian.

Murderous outbreaks of violence finally erupted in June through August 1391 against the Jews in such regions of Spain as Castile, Catalonia, Aragon, Andalucia and Navarre; and major cities: Seville, Toledo, Alicante, Barcelona, Burgos, Palma and Valencia. Massive killings and carnage occurred throughout the cities of Spain and in the offshore islands. Four thousand Jews were killed in Seville alone. In many cities in Spain Jews were converted to Catholicism by forced baptisms. If one chose not to be baptized, the penalty was death. Large proportions of the Jewish population in Barcelona were converted, killed or driven into the countryside. An orgy of violence exploded, with entire communities being exterminated. In Castile mobs ravaged and killed Jews without any governmental control. While estimates vary widely, and are still being assessed, it is believed that during the year long riots over 100,000 were converted, nearly 100,000 murdered and 100,000 saved by going into hiding or fleeing into other Muslim lands.[4] The Jews were reduced to 25% of their original numbers in Aragon. People were busy killing people "for the greater glory of God." Those who converted to Christianity – and many did either voluntarily or were forced to do so – initially had their lives spared.

In 1411 the Dominican Vincent Ferrer would enter

filled synagogues holding both a Torah and a crucifix, shouting, "Baptism or death." With much enthusiasm Ferrer claimed to have baptized some 35,000 Jews. Both the church and the state (and they were almost one) moved to bring the Jews, one way or another, to Catholicism.

Juan II of Castile told his treasurer who had been converted to Catholicism, "Whereas I have been informed that members of your family were, when Jews, considered to be noble, it is right that you be held in even more honor now that you are Christians."[5]

Most of the baptisms were done by forceful coercion. Catholic canon law considers a forced conversion binding and "indelible" for the individuals, even though it may have been done without consent, or even under extreme opposition. According to church law, these forced *conversos* (converted Jews) were nevertheless considered full and equal members of existing Spanish Christian society. Over the ensuing decades there were continued outbreaks of massed forced baptisms along with many voluntary conversions – some undertaken as the only way to survive. Some "voluntary" conversions were the means of staying alive by frightened victims, believing that they eventually would be able to return to Judaism. Other individuals were probably more pragmatic in their outlook and saw conversion as a way to open social and economic doors and as a necessary step to prosper economically.

The baptisms, whatever their varied cause, created a new group in Spain and later in Portugal called *Cristianos Nuevos* or New Christians (those baptized either voluntarily or forcibly). The Jews used the term *Anusim* (forced or coerced ones), while the Spanish used the term *Marranos* (pigs, or swine) as a term of derision. Conversos had been baptized, and were therefore considered New Christians, and Catholics according to the church. Crypto-Jews is a term used for those New Christians who were baptized, and were outwardly appearing to be practicing Christians, but were actually secretly maintaining Jewish practices. There were also over 250,000 Christianized Muslims, who like many Jews, were either converted by force, or voluntarily chose to be baptized, and were known as Moriscos.

Many "voluntary" conversions continued after the temporary cessation of the riots of 1391. About 50,000 additional Jews had been added through baptism to the New Christian population by 1415.[6] Over time a great many of the newly baptized became true practicing Christians and lost their Jewish identity. Further, some of these New Christians used their new found religion in aiding themselves. When they rose in political or religious power they chose to inflict harsh rules and punishments on their former religious brethren. An example of this is Solomon Halevi, who as Paulus de Santa Maria, rose as a New Christian to be Bishop of Cartegena and chancellor of the Kingdom of Castile. He took the lead in baiting his former coreligionists and was responsible in 1412 for some of the most anti-Jewish laws.

But some Jews did not truly convert. They were outwardly Christians, but in their privacy retained their Orthodox Jewish religion and ties as best they could. Many feigned conversion. It was extraordinarily important – of truly life threatening importance – to be certain of the people who knew of ones decision to maintain Judaism. Of course we are talking of a continuing period over generations.

The riots and baptisms throughout Spain waxed and waned, as did the strength of the Reconquista, over many centuries. It was a monumental (almost superhuman) task to maintain both faiths – including required marriages and burials by priests – and yet retain a Jewish heritage and a semblance of religious structure not knowing whom to trust. Essentially both your life and that of your family were literally at stake in more ways than one. The extensive 1391 riots were followed by additional large massacres against Jews in 1411. Toledo saw riots in 1449 and Córdoba once more in 1473 during Purim. In 1412 the Bishop of Burgos (a former Jew) established a series of laws that seriously impacted the already weakened economic position of Jews, and forced them to wear red badges, special clothing and to have long hair and beards. Hatred was seething throughout the land.

Spaniards viewed the New Christians as a new class of people that were rapidly integrating into their social, commercial and business activities. Some Old Christians desired to put those that had just been newly converted into a separate Christian category, but this was rejected by the church hierarchy, as it could be seen as "dividing the body of Christ." The church's position was clear, there being no distinction between a "New Christian" and the preexisting "Old Christians." Those termed New Christians had all the rights and privileges of any other Catholic – as baptism was a permanent, indelible and irreversible act. Further, Pope Nicolas V stated, in a papal pronouncement on October 24, 1449, that the act of baptism (whether forced or voluntary) makes all men Christian regardless of their origins. (Regarding conversion, Rabbi Solomon ben Isaac, known as Rashi, a preeminent Jewish scholar and interpreter of Jewish religious law and texts who lived from 1040 to 1105, wrote that even the act of conversion would not convert Jews from their faith. One still remained a Jew.) And Maimonides, as well, believed that Jews forced to convert remained Jews.

Some of the New Christians found ready entrance to Spanish society and business. They were able with their talent, drive, intelligence and knowledge, to rise rapidly in many fields, such as the judiciary, government, international trade, academia, finance and even the church. Those who were affluent married into the highest of Spanish society, with converts having the advantage of being accepted (at least initially), on equal terms with Christian elite, and competing on equal terms in commerce. The King of Aragon stated that the baptism of the Jews without their consent "was a terrible crime" and "if they do not convert completely and with good will the confusion afterwards will be worse than before."[7] Little did he realize how right he was!

Many of the newly baptized were clearly not true believers in Christianity, and were in the minds of the Catholic hierarchy heretics against the Catholic religion. Many Iberians saw a very large number of people of uncertain religious beliefs becoming deeply entrenched in their social, business and political structure. For example, in the late 15th century, conversos in Cuenca held 85% of the posts in the city council. There also developed a fairly rich, well connected converso class that had risen to elite positions in the church hierarchy itself. In January 1449 a taxation revolt in Toledo quickly evolved into an attack on converso merchants. Some areas, Toledo for example, attempted to enact an edict prohibiting New Christians from public office.

The Spanish people, nobility and church had through the years of anti-Jewish riots and forced baptisms driven many into Christianity. Now they faced the overwhelming dilemma of finding out who was a "true" Christian, and who was a heretic to the new religion that had been forced on them. And, of course, it was not difficult for a non-practicing Jew, following baptism, to be an equally insincere, non-practicing Christian. To further add complexity to an already complex situation, there were a large number of marriages over the years where some of the highest-ranking Spanish Catholic families clearly had Jewish or Moorish ancestors.

But there was one marriage in 1469 that would have lasting impact on Jews, Muslims, Spain, Portugal and on world history. That was the marriage of Isabella to Ferdinand on October 19, 1469 in Valladolid. Ferdinand,

18, and Isabella, 19, had met four days before, but the marriage was carefully planned to gain political advantages if everything fell in place in the years ahead. Ferdinand was King of Sicily, but of more importance was heir to the throne of Aragon, and Isabella to the throne of Castile. If all went as planned they would, when married, have separate thrones, but would together control large parts of Spain. Isabella's attainment of the Castilian throne was far from easy following her brother's death. A five-year civil war ensued, as there was another claimant – Juana la Beltraneja, purported to be her brother's daughter. She would have the next claim on the throne. Isabella and others declared Juana illegitimate, but the daughter had powerful allies in France. However, in the end, Isabella was victorious.

Isabella was a powerful marriage partner and seemed to control policy, but she and Ferdinand spent considerable effort to present an image of two rulers who ruled with one purpose. Although they devoted considerable time in their own dominions, they both looked towards restricting the rights and privileges of the aristocracy, certainly not for any democratic purposes, but to better control the well connected, entrenched power base of the upper classes.

In a like manner, and over many years, the monarchs sought to gain increased control over the powerful Spanish Catholic Church, for the church was not only a center of vast wealth and power, but had a significant control over the population through dogmatic authority and through rituals and sermons. Ferdinand and Isabella continually sought to increase and solidify the power of their monarchial rule. The monarchs' belief in Catholicism was strong, real, and fervent, and they sought as well to raise the church's moral standards and somehow reduce both the financial abuses committed by the clergy and the privileges they assumed. In 1494 Pope Alexander VI simply called them the "Catholic Kings."

Besides the monarchy's concern with the Jews, there still remained the problem of Muslim Granada in southern Spain. A surrender of Granada to Christian Spain was agreed to in 1491, with the Muslims being assured that they would be allowed to maintain their customs, dress and religion. But such ecumenical plans simply could not survive the Catholic religious movement of that time. Not surprisingly, shortly after the agreement there were growing efforts by the Catholic church to forcefully impose conversions and mass baptisms on the Muslims. Within ten years most Muslims had converted (or had been converted) to Moriscos, and Granada was effectively Christian. The Reconquista of Spain was in place.

THE BEGINNING OF THE SPANISH INQUISITION AND HOW IT OPERATED

An application had been made to Rome by the monarchs in 1478 for permission to conduct an Inquisition against heretics to the Catholic religion. The ultimate purpose was to weed out heretical New Christians (people who had been baptized willingly or unwillingly, but were not truly professing or practicing the faith). When permission was granted by Pope Sixtus IV, a royal council – the *Consejo de la Suprema y General Inquisition* was formed in 1483, one of its purposes being the uncovering of Marranos whom they believed were Judaisers or crypto-Jews (New Christians still practicing Judaism after conversion to Christianity). As baptized "Christians" they faced the new risk of being subject to ecclesiastical discipline if found to be heretics to the Christian religion.

The focus of the inquisitors included coercing the individual to admit to serious crimes such as: blasphemy against Christians or the church; apostasy; helping relapsed New Christians return to Judaism; usury; and proselytizing and helping to convert Christians and Moriscos to Judaism.

In the inquisitional inquiries there was much false

testimony given by neighbors, people driven by hatred, greed and jealously, with possible monetary and property enrichment in sight. (There are direct parallels to the Germany of World War II, and to the Soviet show trials against Jews under Stalin). The witnesses against the supposed Marranos were given more advantages than in any secular court as their names were concealed. Arrest meant immediate confiscation of goods. An inventory was kept by notaries, with property held to the end of the trial. In addition, there were people who knew of New Christians who were practicing Judaism secretly, and blackmailed them under threat of exposure.

One significant legal instrument of the Spanish Inquisition was the right, according to the church, to pursue escapees outside local jurisdictions if they wished. Thus, Spain could pursue "fugitives" and try to return them from other colonies and countries. (New information is now coming to light as a result of the rather meticulous records maintained by the Inquisition.)

Tomas de Torquemada (of Jewish descent) became the Inquisitor-General of Castile and Aragon in October 1483, and was one of the most aggressive and oppressive individuals directing the Inquisition.[8] He was largely responsible for most emphatically advising Ferdinand and Isabella to expel the Jews.[9] He was their Catholic confessor, and spoke vehemently in countering ongoing Jewish protestations presented to the Spanish court to reconsider the planned expulsion of Jews in 1492. He was known for the cruelty of the procedures he devised, and the rigor of their enforcement, and was in an excellent position to assure there was no flagging of enthusiasm for the Inqusition. Despite all the horror and turmoil that was occurring, Jewish intellectual activity amazingly continued. Adin Steinsaltz notes that the first printed Talmud appeared in Guadalajara, Spain in 1492.

Between the fear and sorrow of conversion or the

penalty of death, many conversos led a harrowing life. Initially, the Inquisition was focused mainly on New Christians. For example, 99% of those tried (with the use of torture) by the Barcelona tribunal between 1488 and 1505, and 91% of those tried in Valencia between 1484 and 1530 were conversos of Jewish origin.[10] But over time, the Inquisitions concerns included other groups: Moors, backsliding Christians and Protestants. And what we would now call a most egregious form of ethnic cleansing, Archbishop Francisco Ximénez of Toledo was reported to say in January 1500 that "there is now no one in the city who is not a Christian, and all mosques are churches."[11]

At a later time, as the Spanish and Portuguese empire went world-wide, even crypto-Buddhists, crypto-Hindus and crypto-Indians were some of their varied targets. Spain's leading prelate, the Archbishop of Toledo, was brought up on a charge of heresy because he was eating meat on a forbidden day. To show the extent of the madness, an uneducated woman in Toledo in 1568 claimed "all those who die go straight to heaven." She was then accused of heresy for denying the existence of purgatory. Philip II, King of Spain, on speaking of punishing people he knew, stated, "I would bring the wood to burn my own son, if he was as wicked." Religious purity had turned into an obsessive belief.

Torture was used during the questioning tribunal to extract confessions, but not used as the final, eventual punishment. The torturers were, generally, the public executioners who worked for the civil courts, picking up some extra work. The confiscation of one's property could occur after death, even if there were no earlier accusations of heresy. The accusation for most conversos was for "Judaizing," the practice of following Judaism covertly.

Many in the Inquisition would use their power to confiscate property as a means to personally feather their own nests. In addition to obtaining other people's property and land, there was a desire to make the Inquisition a self-supporting activity, with a reduced need for the approval of state or church funding. A resident stated: "They burn only the well off because they have property." Another, indicating that the poor should have less concern, said, "Don't be afraid of being burnt; they're only after the money."

Except for waiting for trial and/or torture there was generally little jail time given as a sentence, as the maintenance of penal facilities was probably too expensive a proposition. Although there were some jail sentences in certain areas, confinement was generally in the prisoners' house, a monastery or a hospital. The church hierarchy announced the punishments generally at autos-da-fé ("actions of faith" in Portuguese), which were elaborately staged punishment spectacles proceeded by grand processions. It sometimes turned into theater, entertainment for the masses, such as the executions that took place in England during the 16th century. One auto-da-fé in Vallodolid, Spain lasted 12 hours with thousands in attendance – (but this was one where the King attended, so it may have been more elaborately orchestrated than normal). The first public burning of heretics was in 1481. But the Inquisition transferred the unfortunate people to the civil (lay) authorities to carry out the punishment, as the church was prohibited from the shedding of blood![12]

The Inquisition had periods of furious activity and periods of quiet dependent on those in charge at the time and the funds available. In some periods it had to be self-supporting. With little confiscated revenue coming in those involved in the Inquisition had to go out looking for conversos who would be targeted to keep the local organization running. One comment to Charles V in 1538 was, "Your Majesty should above all provide that the expenses of the Holy Office (Inquisition) do not come from the property of the condemned, because it is a repugnant thing if inquisitors cannot eat unless they burn." But this is exactly what happened. In 1554 the Inquisitor, Dr. Ramirez, stated, ". . .with a bit of care there will no lack of business whereby God our Lord will be served and the Holy Office be able to sustain itself."[13]

In time, the Inquisition was nearly a worldwide phenomena. Friars were placed aboard most Spanish ships to determine the "religious health" of those on board. You could enter the colonies with any disease, but your religious health would have to meet set standards. The Inquisition eventually reached all the Spanish colonies. Early in the Inquisition those considered for questioning (including torture) were sent back to Spain for their "judicial" tribunal. However, at a later time, many of the tribunals (which were the formal inquisitorial processes) and autos-da-fé took place in the colonies. The Inquisition, which started in Spain in the 1480s, was not ended by the Spanish until 1813. But, unfortunately, it was re-established in 1814, and finally concluded in 1834. This was an amazing span of some 350 years!

The expulsion of the Jews in 1492 caused a loss of one-third or more of the wealthy trading class, and the Spanish economy rapidly spiraled downward. Spain was completely blinded by the glitter of the riches and the plunder coming in from the colonies and pirating on the seas. Spain never seriously concerned itself with modernizing its internal manufacturing or its shipbuilding capabilities; they relied heavily on the new colonies. Despite prodigious wealth flowing into the country, little was used to strengthen and broaden the Spanish economy. Many including the church and a growing bureaucracy simply lived off the incoming torrent of gold, silver and jewels from the New World. Goods were increasingly purchased elsewhere, as the Spanish infrastructure and economy deteriorated. It was a country of world-wide colonies that was growing increasingly dependent on others, and over the coming one and one-half centuries, the country gradually diminished in world importance as its colonies failed or were lost.

World history has shown many times over that a scapegoat will be sought to "explain" failures. There were then feelings in Spain that the country's increasing problems were due to the Jews now outside of Spain, who were acting to undermine the Spanish world-wide activity, and were "stabbing the (Spanish) empire in the back."[14] This was one of many cases of seeing the victim as the cause of the problem. In line with this Phillip II stated that all the heresies in France and Germany were caused by the descendents of Jews.

The rate of capital punishment was higher through history in the Portuguese Inquisition than the Spanish Inquisition. Portugal tried a consistently higher number of Judaizers for heresy than Spain. In fact there was a flow back of conversos from Portugal to Spain in 1630 due to the harshness of Portuguese trial and punishments. In any event the anti-Jewish riots by the Spanish and Portuguese population far exceeded the deaths by the formal Inquisition process. And throughout the Inquisition's history, there was major involvement by the Spanish people. Visitors at the time were impressed by the mass participation of the population in many of the riots and autos-da-fé. Opponents of the Inquisition in Spain also commented on the lack of evidence of any significant opposition. Clearly, in the 15th and 16th centuries, the immense majority of the Spanish people, with their king, magistrates, church and courts, gave their decisive support to the proceedings of the Inquisition.

But Spain had concerns other than the Jews and the Moslems. The country at that time was far from what tourists are treated to now, when visiting the Alhambra and the Gardens of Generalifé in Granada. Seville, for example, was a starving city with many hostile factions, and a host of unremitting hatreds continually boiling to the surface. One description pictured the city as "Unhappy Seville bathed in blood of children..." Galicia was enslaved by lords who secularized (stole) revenues of the church, and by nobles who terrorized villages and forced tributes from the inhabitants. In Andalucia factions contended for power, and attracted thieves and others, giving "license to every appetite, and provoked violent men to murder and assassination."

The Spanish and Portuguese Inquisitions were, unfortunately, not the only frenzy of hatred going on in Europe. In the 45 months between February 1555 and November 1558, 283 Protestants were burned alive in England by Catholic Queen Mary Tudor (Bloody Mary) for heresy. The papal authorities were also very busy monitoring intellectual activities. At a later time Galileo Galilei was called to Rome and warned not to uphold or teach the Copernicus heliocentric (sun-centered) planetary system. Again, certain ideas were seen as dangerous to the faith. He was convicted in 1633; not until 1992 did the Vatican reverse the conviction. All these persecutions (and countless more throughout history), were motivated by religious absolutism, everyone having unalterable and absolute certainty that they were doing God's work on earth.

2

THE SPANISH AND PORTUGUESE EXPULSIONS

In 1492 King Ferdinand and Queen Isabella expelled all Jews from Spain, allowing them 120 days (March 30-July 30, 1492) to sell their possessions (for a pittance) and end their stay of over a thousand years in the country. No gold or silver could be removed (but there were the ever present border guards who could willingly be bribed). The day of expulsion was Tisha b'Av, (the Ninth of Av), the Jewish holy day of fasting commemorating the destruction of the first Temple by Nebuchadnezzar (king of Babylonia) in 586 BCE, and the second Temple by the Romans in 70 CE. Tisha b'Av was also the day of expulsion of Jews from England in 1290. England was the first European country to completely expel Jews from its territory. In that same year the Jews of southern Italian cities were subject to forced baptism.

The previously converted New Christians did not have to leave Spain. (Remember the church position regarding New Christians being equal to existing Old Christians.) Over 250,000 Spanish Jews were impacted by the expulsion order. About 150,000 left the country; 100,000 were baptized in order to remain. The appropriation of Jewish property and the transference of ownership to others (as was done in Germany and Poland), may have been a sop to calm some of the festering concerns of the Spaniards against many of the unpopular policies of the monarchy.

The written expulsion edict stated that the monarchs believed that the unconverted Jews were a terrible influence on the New Christians and were the main cause of their being led astray – away from Christianity and back to Judaism. In addition, Isabella wanted the forced conversion of the Moors. The last remnant of Muslim rule in Spain was in Granada, and that fell to the Christians in 1492. The driving force to wipe out "heresy" was Isabella who was fanatically devoted to Catholicism and its rites. Her fervor was highly focused on ridding Spain of the Moors and Jews. To her they were the primary forces opposing Jesus and Christianity in the past, and she saw these peoples as hostile to the Christian cross and, from her perspective, being rid of these two groups (or having them converted to Catholicism) was clearly the answer.

Part of the original 1492 text clearly spells out the thoughts that Isabella, Torquemada and Ferdinand had regarding the Jews in undertaking the expulsion:

> ". . .we are informed by the Inquisitors and many other religious persons, ecclesiastical and secular, it is evident and apparent that the great damage to the Christians has resulted from and does result from the participation, conversation and communication that they have had with the Jews, who try to always achieve by whatever ways and means possible to subvert and to draw away faithful Christians from our holy Catholic faith and to separate them from it, and to attract and pervert them to their injurious belief and opinion, instructing them in their ceremonies and observances of the Law, trying to circumcise them and their children, giving them books from which to read prayers, and declaring that they ought to fast, and joining with them to read and teach the histories of their Law; notifying them of Passover before it comes, advising them what they should observe and do, giving them and taking unto them the unleavened bread and (ritually) slaughtered meats with the ceremonies, instructing them on the things they should stay away from, thus in the food as in other matters, for observance of the Law, and persuading them as much as they can there is no other law or truth besides

> it. This is evident from the many declaration and confessions (obtained) as much from the Jews themselves as from those perverted and deceived by them, which has redounded to the great injury, detriment and opprobrium of our holy Catholic faith."[1]

The expulsion order dramatically intensified the converso problem without solving it. Over one half of the Jews in Spain converted to Christianity.[2] These Jews were essentially forced into Christian society. All Jewish books were confiscated. Many Jews chose baptism during the four month "grace" period. Baptism was the means of remaining in Spain with their possessions and family. In effect their choice other than emigration was to hide their true religion under the cover of Christianity, or as many did to truly and permanently change their faith. Of course this increased the New Christian population, and the question was who was a true Christian and who a heretic.

Jews also had to leave Sardinia, and about 37,000 Jews had to leave Sicily in 1493. Both were then under Spanish domination. Additionally, tens of thousands of Jews went to adjacent Portugal under a temporary family entrance permit (generally 8 months) if they could pay the heavy governmental fee of 10 gold crusados (besides any bribery involved). Others went to Morocco, Algeria, Egypt, Palestine, the Balkans, parts of Italy, the Ottoman Empire (Turkey), Hamburg, and later, many eventually poured into Protestant Amsterdam where they found a welcome haven. The Ottoman Empire accepted large numbers of Jews, clearly understanding the social and economic importance and the strengths of the Spanish Jews. The Ottoman Sultan Bayazid II on hearing of the massive expulsion of Jews commented, "Can such a man be wise – one who impoverished his Kingdom while enriching my own." (The words proved prophetic, as Spain was to pay an intellectual and economic price for centuries to come.) The fact that Jews left for other countries did not necessarily end their strife. Most countries welcomed them, but giving only one example, refugee Jews from Spain were burned at the stake in Dubrovnik in 1502. In many countries they paid heavy bribes to be allowed to stay.[3]

The relatively safe haven of Spanish Jews in Portugal did not last. King John II of Portugal had promised ships would be available to other countries, but few vessels appeared: people were hurried on board in Lisbon and Oporto, brutally treated by the crew and dumped onto the African coast, some sold into slavery and many others dying on the African coast.[4] King John died in 1495 succeeded by King Manuel I, who eased some of the rules against Jews, but this more tolerant attitude dramatically changed when a marriage between the young Portuguese King and Isabel was planned. Isabel was the daughter of Isabella and Ferdinand, and their only son had died.

Through this new marriage a union between Spain and Portugal was to be established. Isabel, their daughter, was a sister of Katharine of Aragon, King Henry VIII's first wife. One crucially important condition was set by the Spanish monarchy that would dramatically affect Jewish history. Isabel declared she would not set foot on Portuguese soil, or marry, unless Portugal was cleansed of the "accursed" Jews as her mother had done.[5] This is another example how major points in history can turn on most unexpected events. The marriage contract was signed on November 30, 1496 and the Portuguese edict of expulsion of December 25, 1496 gave Jews ten months to leave. The order (paraphrasing the Spanish declaration) declared, "The Jews persist in their hatred of the Holy Catholic Faith; they commit crimes against the religion and deflect Christians from the path of truth."[6] King Manuel readily accepted their demand as he would not put his kingdom in jeopardy in order to respond to the concerns of the Jews.

While these dramatic events that would harshly impact Jewish life were unfolding, Spain and Portugal were envisioning their controlling large areas of the globe. In apparent response to a bull by Pope Alexander VI in 1493, Spain and Portugal established the Treaty of Tordesillas in 1494 that set about dividing the non-Christian world into two areas of influence. The treaty initially gave the vast majority of the New World to Spain, with Africa and India going to Portugal. The geographic boundaries drawn allowed Portugal to claim Brazil some six years after the treaty. Shortly after this treaty, Vasco da Gama traveled around Africa and the Cape of Good Hope to India, giving Portugal vast wealth in the spice trade.

These details reveal that the self-inflicted "Jewish problem" was but one of many ongoing issues of these two countries, both of which were then major sea powers. They both saw large parts of the world as their domain.

Despite all this activity related to the marriage, King Manuel actually did not desire to lose the Jewish community and the large economic base that they contributed as businessmen, traders, artisians, scientists and authors. Nor did he want to lose the great number of recent immigrants who had entered from Spain.[7] The king first attempted a policy of forcible conversions, which he thought the Jews would accept (considering the alternatives), as the basis for their staying in Portugal. The newly baptized New Christians were forbidden to leave, while unbaptized Jews and Moors had to leave by October 1497. This policy would, he thought, keep a high percentage of the Jews in the country. By forcing the newly baptized Jews to stay, Manuel believed he would meet both his economic needs as well as cleverly provide a loophole around the marriage stipulation. The Jews would certainly see where their best interests lay, and would remain "voluntarily."

This disastrous policy failed. Jews who had left Spain for Portugal, and other Jews within Portugal, started to leave as best they could, under the most dire circumstances.

Again, some did choose baptism (either forcibly or "voluntarily") in an attempt to maintain their lives. Many children 4 to 14 were captured and forcibly baptized which caused the parents to convert in order to remain in the country with their children. In 1506, in one of many horrific cases over the years, word was spread that ships were being readied in Lisbon to take Jews out of the country. When some 20,000 arrived at the designated site near a palace in Lisbon, they were trapped, denied food and water and were forcibly baptized. Two thousand Jews were killed at this site. The king, trying to distance himself from what was occurring, punished the perpetrators of the massacre. All Jews in Portugal essentially were envisioned as becoming New Christians by this failed policy, and from these unfortunate Spanish and Portuguese Jews grew the worldwide movement of Sephardic Jews that would, in time, be seen in the New World.

There is a story (possibly apocryphal) reflecting the significant amount of intermarriage that had taken place over the many years in Portugal and Spain. As the King of Portugal was to sign the edict of expulsion of the Jews, his minister said to the king, "When they go, who should go first, you or me?" King Manuel died in 1521.

The establishment of an inquisition in Portugal and the methods of carrying it out had to be approved in Rome – and in some cases the approval process was quite lengthy. Manuel's successor, King John III, tried over many years to get the approval, and he finally succeeded with Pope Paul III in 1536. The Vatican proclamations of 1536, 1539 and 1547 then set the stage for a Portuguese Inquisition starting in 1541.[8] Autos-da-fé took place in Lisbon, Coimbra and Evora during the next 30 years. Crypto-Jews were even returning to Spain, their home, hoping the Inquisition would not be as active in that country. Thousands of very courageous Jews had gone to various colonies such as Brazil, Peru, Mexico, Chile and Bolivia, despite the fact that there were harsh restrictions against them going, except if exiled as punishment. Neverthless, "unconverted" Jews and many New Christians viewed these colonies as areas where there could be greater opportunities to start their lives anew, away from the unending European religious hatreds. Additionally, the Inquisition was generally found to be weaker, and not as pervasive, in the initial years after its establishment in the new colonies. It took time for the Inquisition's bureaucracy to gain strength overseas, as well as to gain needed Vatican approval.

In particular, Jews went to Brazil despite highly restrictive laws against such travel. Brazil was a huge, rugged, wild and deeply forested country that appeared to have economic potential, and some protection in its vast geographic area from the Inquisition. Over the coming years many went to Brazil as New Christians, permanently leaving Judaism. But some remained as crypto-Jews, covertly practicing Judaism, hoping in time to regain an opportunity to openly practice their original religion.

In 1580 Portugal became part of the Spanish Empire, and being a clandestine Jew became even more dangerous as the Inquisition gained intensity. The church sent agents to roam Brazil and other countries, and some Jews who tried to escape were shipped back to the Iberian Peninsula for trial.

The Catholic Church's trials and punishments continued in Spain with waves of persecutions into the 18th century. In the 1730s there were grand autos-da-fé in Madrid, Mallorca, Granada and Seville; one of the final ones took place in Toledo in 1756. This reduction of events cannot be attributed to a growing religious tolerance, but rather to the sad fact that the Jewish population was decimated and effectively eliminated from Spain. The Spanish even tried to have the British restrict Jews and Muslims from living in the captured territory of Gibralter, where so long ago Tarik ibn Ziyad had crossed into Spain.

The Inquisition has now faded into history. But some are now trying to minimize its horrors, impact and importance. Most others see the murders, baptisms and expulsions as part of an ongoing global, brutal historical pageant of religious conflict, anti-Semitism, terrorism and unbridled and irrational hatred. Governmental authorities in the 19th and 20th centuries have managed to easily destroy far, far greater numbers of people than died in the Spanish and Portuguese Inquisitions.

There were attempts to shift blame on whether the Inquisition was driven by the church or by the state. The ecclesiastics determined both the offenses and the punishment; secular authorities assumed responsibility for the rest. It was truly a joint effort. The Inquisition was a product of its time, but, unfortunately, its heritage of religious-based conflict remains in place, and is an active and ongoing worldwide activity to this day.

The direct result of the turmoil and tragedy of the Spanish and Portuguese Inquisitions was that it lastingly changed world Jewry, setting in motion an unprecedented movement of Jews across the globe. It also set the stage for a major expansion of Jewish involvement in world trade and commerce. And over time, it would bring Jews to areas of the world where, after endless centuries of turmoil, they hoped to find religious tolerance, and economic and social equality.

3

SPANISH AND PORTUGUESE DIASPORA AND MIGRATION TO THE WESTERN HEMISPHERE

At the beginning of the 16th century Spain and Portugal were at the height of their global exploration and colonial development (1415-1808). The Dutch were engaged in world exploration between 1660 through about 1800. These countries were sailing the world in a frenzy of historic voyages of exploration, and they established colonies and areas of control in the Philippeans, India (Goa), China, Africa, the Spice Islands, and Central and South America. After the Iberian expulsions there were significant Jewish migration to Morocco, Algeria, Palestine, Egypt, the Ottoman Empire (Turkey), portions of Italy, Navarre, France, the Balkans, Hamburg, India, Salonica and Timor.

In the late 1550s Philip II of Spain brought the Inquisition to the Netherlands, and attempted to make the Low Countries a Spanish province. But there was major opposition to both Spanish control and attempts to impose Catholicism on a population that desired greater religious and economic autonomy. By 1570 the northern provinces of the Netherlands wrested control from Spain, but the south remained mostly under Spanish Catholic rule until 1648.

Despite the long continuing wars, the Protestant Low Countries were welcoming Jews, Huguenots and others. Sephardim came from both Spain and Portugal to Amsterdam in the late 16th century; Ashkenazim emigrated from Germany, Hungary and Poland in the early 1600s. The latter were generally not educated or well off financially, and did not readily integrate into Dutch society or commerce. Yet, Amsterdam became a most important haven for both groups. Sephardic Jews considered themselves superior to their bretheren from central and eastern Europe. There was little mixing or association. The Sephardic, generally richer, carefully maintained the social class distinctions that had been their custom in Spain and Portugal.

Although they could not enter the closed guild system, the Sephardim, within a brief time, became deeply involved in the business activity of the city. The first Jew to gain Dutch citizenship was a Sephardi in 1597.

The Sephardim invested in the Dutch East India Company (chartered in 1602) and the Dutch West India Company (chartered in 1621). By the mid 1600s the Sephardim were major shareholders in both organizations, which had become trading and colonizing companies charted by the States-General of the Dutch republic, and had almost complete administrative and judicial powers over the overseas colonies in their charge.

One Dutchman stated, "Christian merchants found themselves in the role of spectators of the Israelite businesses." Alan Taylor notes that by 1670 the Dutch had more shipping than Spain, France and England combined.

The Sephardim, in particular, were an integral part of a growing commercial sector that would flourish with the expansion of banking, shipping and international trade in a large array of commodities. It was the beginning of a golden period of Jewish activity. Their movement in the Netherlands came at a fortuitous time, when the Dutch were broadening their economic reach through major programs of world-wide exploration and colonization. This warm environment allowed the recently harried Sephardim to develop more active civic, commercial and religious lives, protected from religious persecution. A strong Jewish base was created in Amsterdam that would eventually play a key role in the seeding of a Jewish diaspora throughout the Western Hemisphere, as well as in the movement of Jews back to England.

The Netherlands gave civic rights to non-Christians and allowed them to participate in commercial activities, as well as allowing the open practice of non-Christian religions. These were firsts in Europe. Jews in Amsterdam were able to develop their lives to their full capability, free from the ever-present religious and social persecution. By 1700 there were close to 8,000 Jews in Amsterdam.

The Ashkenazim undertook to build an attached complex of four synagogues: the Grote Synagogue in 1671; Obbene Shul in 1685; Niewe Synagogue in 1752, and Dritt Shul in 1778. (This complex is now a Museum of Jewish Culture, detailing the history of Jews in the Netherlands.) The Sephardim's Great Portuguese Synagogue was opened in 1675.

The Ashlenazi synagogue complex and the Portuguese synagogue are now just a short walk apart across Weesperstaat. In 1723 Roeland van Louve wrote a very simple but clearly heartfelt poem that captured some of his feeling about his city and its people aiding the Jews:

> Our city fathers deserve great praise,
> For letting men worship in different ways
> Be they Romans or not, be they Christians or Jews,
> Who their splendid Portuguese church may choose,
> Or the fine smaller church across the way,
> Where the German Jews worship as in Moses' day.

BRAZIL AND THE NEW WORLD

A major event that would in time impact the movement of Jews to the Western World was Pedro Alvarez Cabral's discovery of Brazil in 1500, during his westward voyage to India. The establishment of this new Portuguese colony would play a most dramatic role in the coming years for many Jews attempting to escape the Iberian Peninsula. Of course, there were other truly significant events at that time – such as the earlier voyages by Christopher Columbus to the New World. Whether Columbus' family, somewhere along the line, had a converso past still remains uncertain.

Simon Wiesenthal, Robert Fuson and Salvador de Madariaga, among many others, have waded in to address their theories of why, what and when regarding the possible Jewish link to the Admiral of the Seas (which was one of Columbus' eventual titles). Columbus himself was a master in concealing, and better yet, obfuscating his background, not only of his family and birthplace, but of other important activities as well. In addition, the loss and sale of many of Columbus' documents by his grandson has added to great unknowns in the historic record, and has frustrated historians. But these many gaps and uncertainties have also given a chance to a number of people to contrive a host of theories and speculation that still swirl around Columbus to this day.

Columbus was a practicing Catholic and his writings are continually seeded with many Christological references, and references to Mary and the Saints. Almost all historians believe he was born around 1451 in Genoa. However, some items of possible general interest should be mentioned. His navigator and two or three others on his first voyage appear to have been Jews, or at least conversos. Some funding of the voyages appear to have involved Jewish connections, such as Luis de Santangel (a converso) and Gabriel Sanchez, who were important personages in the Spanish treasury. (On Columbus' return in March 1493 his first letter about the voyage went to Santangel.) Some maps and nautical instruments aboard the ships were most probably the products of Jehudah Cresques, a Jew who was at one time head of the Nautical Academy of Palma.[1]

And Abraham Zacuto, a Spanish astronomer and historian, wrote material on astronomy that was translated into Spanish and Latin, and prepared astronomical tables for navigational use at that time.[2] (Later, Zacuto went to Tunis and finished his Sepher Yuhasin on the history of rabbinic scholarship.) Luis de Torres, a baptized Jew, travelled with Columbus. He was their translator and is believed to be the first person to trod on the new land.

It appears that Columbus had such instruments as astrolabs and quadrants on board to determine latitude, but did not rely on them. According to Robert Fuson, the major method used was dead reckoning. Other navigational methods included the compass; throwing wood overboard at the bow to determine the elapsed time for the ship to pass the floating object, with the short time estimated using rhythmic chants; a 30-minute hourglass to determine the passage of longer periods of time, and celestial fixes when possible.

From Columbus' writings and documentation there is no doubt he was a Christian, however, he would use both Christological and Old Testament references. Here are two examples from his daily shipboard log (translated by Robert Fuson) that were written during the thirty-three day voyage to the New World in 1492. On August 3, 1492 he wrote:

> "In the Name of our Lord Jesus Christ, Most Christian, exalted, excellent and Powerful princes, King and Queen of Spains. . . Therefore, after having banished all the Jews from your Kingdom and realms, during this same month of January Your Highness ordered me to go with sufficient fleet to the said regions of India. . .[3]

At another point in the same log he makes reference to the Old Testament. This took place on September 23, 1492 when his three ships were traveling through the Sargasso Sea:

> "When I get wind from the SW or west it is inconsistent, and that, along with the flat sea, has led the men to believe we will never get home. I told them that we are near land and that is what is keeping the sea smooth. (They would not see land until October 11, 1492-JH). Later, when the sea made up considerably without wind, they were astonished. I saw this as a sign from God, and it was very helpful to me. Such a sign has not appeared since Moses led the Jews out of Egypt, and they dared not lay violent hands on him because the miracle that God had wrought. As with Moses when he led his people out of captivity, my people were humbled by this act of the Almighty."

At this point, I will leave the many enigmas and uncertainties about Columbus that still remain some 500 years after his voyages. Following Cabral's voyage of discovery to Brazil in 1500 a long colonization period followed. Many adventurers, convicts, dregs of society, farmers, traders, minor and important governmental personnel, true Christians, hidden Jews and Jews who had permanently left the faith and some Jews who were exiled due to charges of heresy were going to this "new land" of Brazil. Each group had a reason for emigrating to some of these new colonies. For Jews remaining in the faith these distant areas could just possibly be a safer place for them to rebuild their lives, hopefully free from the clutches of the Inquisition. The Inquisition's bureaucracy was not as yet fully in place in the remote colonies. From 1500 to about 1640 many Marranos came both for economic opportunity and for a chance to be thousands of miles away from the active and spreading tentacles of the Inquisition.

These early movements of Jews were primarily to South America, closely followed by Jews entering Mexico – with a handful coming with the initial landing of Hernando Cortez in the Yucatan in 1519.

South America was a wilderness that could be an

area of opportunity, and to a degree, a haven and refuge. It took longer for the operating bureaucracies to be put in place in the more remote colonies. Additionally, approvals were needed from the pope in Rome for the initiation of the Inquisition. However, the delay did not in any way guarantee long-term safety, as it was known that the Inquisition would surely follow, as it did in all the Portuguese and Spanish colonies. It's just that enforcers were not yet on the scene in adequate numbers.

While the Spanish were very attentive to the "New Christian problem" very early on, it took the Portuguese until about 1549 to establish a body of Jesuits and Franciscans who, in the name of the church, intervened in almost all areas of life. (This was similar to what was done in Southern France in the Middle Ages.) In 1551, a Bishop of Brazil, as well as a Bishop of Salvador, were appointed. From that time on, the Roman Catholic hierarchy tried to establish a European type of religious order in this vast wilderness area. The Inquisition was in place, with powers necessary for inquiry and property confiscation. Churchmen went about Christianizing the native Indians, as well as actively trying to control and train them into passive plantation laborers to aid the struggling economy.

Laboring for the Portuguese was far from easy. The Portuguese grip (as well as the church's grip) was being tightened through the purposeful breaking up of cohesive social units and the institution of slavery. A priest was in every community, and missionaries were sent to all unincorporated villages. The priests began to acquire land and serfs. To control these vast estates a "lordship" class was established that eventually resulted in priests being in the upper economic and social strata of society. Concubinage was common and in the open.

Indians were baptized by the thousands, apparently accepting the new priests who replaced their own. And the church was now tracking New Christian backsliders, who were seen as practicing their former Indian religions – essentially crypto-Indians. The churches grew larger, acquired wealth and were richly decorated. The Jews were just a minute segment of this growing country. But while all this was going on the search for heretics was also on the agenda. And the Jews were most certainly wary of the thousands of eyes ready to turn them in to the ecclesiastical authority with a charge of *heresy.*

In 1503 a small number of ships, led by the Marrano navigator, Fernando de Noronha, approached Brazil and the Brazilian archipelago, which was named for him, located in the Atlantic Ocean some 300 miles northeast of Recife. Some crypto-Jews settled in what would be the northeast Brazilian state of Bahia. Others tried to establish themselves along and near the coastline. Many Jews moved to the interior, only to have their very small settlements burned down, with many more dying of starvation.

Sao Paulo and areas south of the city had the largest Jewish settlement in the early 1550s. They also established a port named Cananéia (after the biblical Canaan), which is still on the map, about 150 miles south of Santos, Brazil.[4] Catholic padres would meet incoming ships and aggressively inquire of the "religious health" of the passengers. Many of them were Old Catholics as well as Marranos who had truly converted to Catholicism. The padres, however, were seeking crypto-Jews and anyone showing the "fatal diseases" of heresy and apostacy.

Jews also went to Chile, Peru and Argentina (landing in the Rio de la Plata, just north of Buenos Aires) in the 16th and 17th centuries. By 1571 many autos-da-fé – the elaborate punishment spectacles held in major squares – were taking place in Mexico City. The Inquisition was in place in Peru in 1596. In time the autos-da-fé were occurring in Lima in such large numbers, and targeting people of importance in the country's economy, that it impacted Peru's economic vitality.

Some 56 accused Marranos died in flames in a huge auto-de-fé in Peru in 1639. Many people burned in the name of "blood purity." It was not the first or the last time that Spain's obsessive focus on religious purity would weaken a colony. Manuel Perez, one of the victims, was purported to be one of the wealthiest men in the country. Jews who were able to escape Peru for Chile were buying citizenship papers at exorbitant fees. Some would adopt Spanish names for protection. Many "Blumenthals" became "Flores."

Initially, those people declared as heretics or crypto-Jews by the local Inquisition were shipped back to Europe for questioning and "trial." Later, the entire process was undertaken in the New World to keep down the costs of the Inquisition and to maintain local control. Many autos-da-fé became local festivals, lighting up the skies in many cities.

At that time countries with strong navies were aggressively searching for poorly defended and sparsely populated colonies, which would be captured for the productive benefit of the motherland. In 1624 when the Dutch captured Bahia from the Portuguese, Jews in other Brazilian colonies quickly hastened to the new Dutch territory, hoping to find a civic and religious haven from the Inquisition.

Almost immediately crypto-Jews, many who had lived in Brazil for generations, came out into the open, certainly an exceedingly dangerous practice at that time. Unfortunately, Bahia was recaptured by the Portuguese in less than a year, and many Jews found themselves vulnerable to the Old Christian administrators. But by 1630 the Dutch regained the territory and a new colony, New Holland, was formed, which included the city of Recife and parts of the northeast Brazilian region of Pernambuco.

A strong community developed, with a large percentage of Jews. Religious activity flourished. As one would expect the Portuguese accused the Jews of instigating the Dutch to capture the colony for them.

New Holland was managed by the Dutch West India Company, headquartered in Amsterdam. This is the same organization that managed New Amsterdam (lower Manhattan Island in New York) and also established the Dutch colony of Curaçao in 1634.

Many Jews continued to settle in New Holland and Recife, as the Dutch proved over time to be very supportive of early Jewish colonizers and immigrants.

After the Dutch establishment of New Holland, Jews came in increasing numbers from Amsterdam, from the Iberian Peninsula and from other parts of Brazil. Close to 1,000 Jews are thought to have been in Recife and in Pernambuco in the early 1630s and the number rapidly increased to as many as 5,000 by the 1640s. It is commonly thought, that over time, the Jews controlled about 60% of the sugar industry and trade, which became the main industrial activity. Other Jews were storekeepers, merchants, sugar brokers, peddlers, traders, exporters, and farmers of many crops including tobacco. The sugar industry included large productive plantations using slave labor – considered a most natural and common way to do business in those times.

To show the extent of Jewish involvement in New Holland, a Spanish document of 1643 complains of the way Jews swarm between the banks of the Amazon and the Orinoco Rivers. There was a Jewish cemetery, a hospice, an elementary school, a cantor and a shochet (ritual slaughterer). Gambling houses were closed on the Sabbath. There was a tax if you chose to leave the colony. Many hidden Jews feeling comfortable in their new home in New Holland came out into the open, no longer hiding their religion. They were so open and public in their practice of Judaism that some believed that they had become too visible and were advised to be a bit more prudent.

Isaac Aboab de Fonseca (1605-1693), the first rabbi

to be in the Western Hemisphere, left his pulpit in Congregation Bet Israel in Amsterdam (which he led when he was only twenty-one) to settle in Recife in 1642.[5] Bringing over 200 congregants with him, he established Kahal Kadosh Zur Yisroel (Holy Congregation Rock of Israel).

The rabbi had been born in Portugal. His family first moved to France and then to the Netherlands. He was an excellent Hebrew poet, translating many cabbalistic writings into Spanish. Additionally, Rabbi de Fonseca was one of the major shareholders in the Dutch West India Co., the trading and colonizing organization. That a rabbi would come and bring people to remote Recife spoke well of the Dutch regard for the potential of this community. (The first ordained rabbi to have a pulpit in America would be Abraham Rice in Baltimore in 1840, nearly 200 years later.)

Another synagogue was erected in Mauricia (near the outer harbor of Recife), named Magen Avraham (Shield of Abraham).

There were also Ashkenazim, as well, who mainly came to Recife from Germany, Hungary, Turkey and Poland by way of Amsterdam. At one point Jews were in the majority in Recife, and there was even a Jewish brigade that was exempt from guard duty on the Sabbath. A Rabbi Raphael Hayim d'Aguilar also came from Amsterdam.

However, by 1645 the Portuguese started a long-term attempt to regain this part of Brazil, with a Portuguese Jesuit Joam Vieyra convincing the Portuguese king of the need to recapture Recife – as the "city was chiefly inhabited by Jews, most of them originally fugitives from Portugal." Besides this religious-based reason, the Portuguese were losing their hold on parts of Asia and felt they needed to get back, in major ways, into the sugar and lucrative slave trading business in Brazil. In addition to this conflict between the Dutch and Portuguese, the Dutch and English were at the same time fighting a series of wars in

1652-1674; the English were trying to destroy the Dutch power in international trade. An English victory would allow England to gain control of the slave trade between Africa and the Americas, as well as the country's desire to seize New Amsterdam from the Dutch. And if not enough was going on, the British were also trying to disrupt Spanish trade routes, especially to Chile.

The Portuguese, during these various power struggles, issued an ultimatum to the Dutch to surrender Recife and Pernambuco. And to add to the Dutch and Jewish settlers' problems, the economy of the area was weakened by drought, resulting in poor sugar crops in 1642-1644. The Jews were offered an amnesty by the Portuguese if they did not support and defend the Dutch and did not aid in protecting the colony. That offer was emphatically turned down; Jews openly and actively supported the Dutch over a long nine year period of sea-borne sieges. The Jews chose to support those who gave them both economic and religious freedom.

Rabbi de Fonseca had Jews from all over the colony rally to the defense of the entire Dutch held areas throughout Pernambuco. Eighteen ships under the command of David Peixotto, a Dutch Jew, brought food and supplies to the now famine stricken area, but a new siege ended the Dutch rule in 1654. When the area fell, the Dutch backed up their friends who supported them, and insisted that as a condition of surrender the Portuguese give amnesty to Jews and other members of the population. The Portuguese agreed to this initially, then turned around and demanded that the Jews leave rapidly. There would be no Jewish community of this size for another 150 years.

Rabbi de Fonseca, and others, returned to Amsterdam, where he became the spiritual leader of Amsterdam's Sephardic community. In 1656 and shortly afterwards, de Fonseca was involved in the excommunication of the philosopher Baruch Spinoza, who, after the excommunication, dropped his Hebrew name and used the Latin form Benedict.

The rapid exodus of the Dutch (and the Jews within the Dutch colony) impacted the economy of Brazil as the Jews, in particular, took both their capital as well as their technical knowledge of the processing, refining and trading of sugar.[6] The Portuguese unsuccessfully tried to retain some of the expertise.

Recife was at that time called the *Port of the Jews.* The old building where a synagogue was located has recently reopened as a museum.

And now we come to a period after the fall of Recife in 1654, where a host of important events took place in different parts of the world that would impact future Jewish history in North America. These include:

— Jews colonizing many Caribbean islands and having major economic impacts on these islands, including their use in a complex network of trade, linking the American colonies with Europe and Africa.

— The historic story of the initial twenty-three Jews entering lower Manhattan Island (New Amsterdam) in 1654 following their expulsion from Recife, and facing the formidable Peter Stuyvesant; and

— Jews reentering London in the 1650s and 1660s after an expulsion lasting some 350 years, and then forming synagogues such as Bevis Marks. Bevis Marks and the Portuguese synagogue in Amsterdam were, for many, the synagogues to emulate. Both synagogues would serve important roles for the American Jewish communities as sources for Torahs, funding, Hebrew talent and immigrants.

REENTERING ENGLAND UNDER OLIVER CROMWELL

Prior to the expulsion of Jews from England in 1290 by Edward I, there was an extended period of extortion of the Jews by the English monarchy, and the imposition of statutes designed to cause economic ruin to the Jewish community. England was among the first to force Jews to wear special badges, and required them to attend conversion sermons. It was also the first European country to expel all their Jews.

In 1290 on the Jewish Day of Mourning for the destruction of the Temple in Jerusalem in 70 CE (Tisha b'Av) about 15,000 were expelled from England. They tried to find homes in Germany, Flanders (the area along the North Sea from Calais to southern Netherlands), Spain and, particularly, France (not anticipating that 16 years later they would be expelled from France).

Jews were not allowed to return to England for another 360 years until the time of Oliver Cromwell in the 1650s. Earlier than that, a small number of Spanish, Portuguese and other Jews would enter, mostly illegally. At times a few were actually invited to immigrate due to their special talents desired by the royal families. In 1410 King Henry IV brought in Dr. Elias Sabot from Italy to serve the king.[7]

Similarly, Dr. Rodrigo Lopez was invited to serve on the staff of St. Bartholomew in 1561; he was later physican to Queen Elizabeth I in 1586. Unfortunately, he was accused of trying to poison the queen and was executed. Another invitee was Joachim Gaunse, a metallurgist from Prague, in 1581, who would be in North Carolina by 1585 as part of the earliest attempted (and failed) British settlement.

England was able to benefit from the Marranos, who supplied the British with information from people they knew in Iberia. It was a time of many naval engagements against Spain, as well as a time of high anti-Spanish feelings. Although useful to the crown, Jews, nevertheless, had to maintain a very low profile in Protestant England.

Mennaseh ben Israel, an Amsterdam rabbi, was deeply involved in trying to allow Jews to enter England. He wrote letters to Cromwell and periodically visited him in the 1650s. He may have been in somewhat of a rush, because he believed that the Messiah would return in 1666, and as few Jews lived in England, their admittance "from the four corners of the earth" would hasten the holy event.

The clergy, English merchants and most of the government were opposed to rescinding the ban on Jews, but not on the basis of the Messiah. In particular there was opposition to business-oriented Sephardim coming in. The passing of the British Navigation Act in 1651, which restricted British trade to the use of British ships, motivated the highly dynamic Dutch Sephardi international trade merchants in Amsterdam to try to enter England and set up commercial branches in London.[8]

Cromwell was not able to get a formal document passed allowing acceptance of Jews in England, but he simply let them in by looking the other way. He stated he would give Jews protection; allow them to enter the commercial marketplace; allow them to practice their religion privately, and allow them to establish a cemetery.

The entrance of Jews set off a host of spurious rumors, one of which was that the Jewish community had put in a bid to buy the recently rebuilt St. Paul's Cathedral and would convert it into a synagogue. In 1656 the growing number of Jews did establish a synagogue on Creechurch Lane, and when that proved to be too small, even though it was enlarged in 1674, they leased a site about one block away on Bevis Marks Street, and built Kahal Kadosh Sharei Hashamayim (Holy Congregation Gates of Heaven) in 1701. This became commonly known as the Bevis Marks synagogue. This building remains and can still be visited.

The importance of Bevis Marks in our discussion is

that this synagogue would be a source of spiritual and financial support to a number of the new Jewish communities in the American colonies. Some members of Bevis Marks funded one-way transportation to some of the early immigrants to the North American colonies – such as some 42 Sephardic and Ashkenazi Jews going to Savannah in 1733. One of the main funders was Joseph Salvador, the first director of the Dutch East India Company as well as president of the Portuguese congregation in London, who had acquired great wealth and purchased significant holdings in South Carolina. The time appeared ripe for the Jewish movement into the Caribbean and into the colonies.

Thus about 160 years after the Spanish and Portuguese expulsion edicts of 1492 and 1497, we now have Sephardi and some Ashkenazi Jews spreading across the Caribbean; a strong population of Sephardim and a growing number of Askenazim in Amsterdam; Jews in Mexico, Central America and South America, including Surinam and Guiana, and Jews entering the east coast of what will be the United States.

4

THE EARLY JEWS IN MEXICO, THE CARIBBEAN AND SOUTHWEST

One of the many results of the expulsion of the Jews from the Iberian peninsula was the presence of Jewish settlers in Mexico after the arrival of Hernando Cortez's small army in 1519. By 1521 the Aztec empire had fallen. Crypto-Jews started coming into Mexico (called New Spain), with some even fighting with Cortez. However, there was a dramatic increase in the activity of the Inquisition in Portugal in 1536 once the pope approved the request for the Inquisition. Large numbers of Jews came to New Spain, (particularly in Mexico City), even though there were strong prohibitions and attempts at the ports to prevent them from coming. Some sources believe that in 1550 there were more crypto-Jews in Mexico City than Spanish Catholics, although others consider the numbers were closer to 20 to 25% of the Catholic population.

Spain tried, ineffectually, to establish controls to stem the movement of New Christians to New Spain – particularly those they thought may be clandestinely practicing Judaism. Emperor Charles V brought the Inquisition and autos-da-fé to Mexico in 1528.[1] One of the first victims was Hernando Alonzo, who had fought for the Spanish with Cortez. Then, for some half a century the crypto-Jews lived fairly quietly in Mexico with minimal activity by the Inquisition directed towards Jews.

By the late 1560s the ever-watchful King Philip II of Spain saw a number of growing problems. One was the defense of his expanding territories. The British Sir Francis Drake was roaming the world plundering Spanish holdings in Valparaiso, Chile and Panama, as well as capturing Spanish ships and their valuable cargos. He even harrassed the Spanish on the west coast of America, using Spanish charts he had "acquired," stopping off at San Francisco to check Spanish activity. But Philip of Spain, amid all these issues, saw one problem that needed his careful attention. He believed that Mexico was being "desecrated by Jews and heretics, principally of Portuguese nationality," and ordered the Inquisition tribunals to be established in New Spain (Mexico).

The Holy Office of the Inquisition then set up an aggressive operation in Mexico City in 1571. Philip was also concerned with Catholics violating Catholic morality – such as bigamy. Major autos-da-fé with much pomp took place in Mexico City in February 1574. From this point in time, over 900 Jews were tried in Mexico during the 16th and 17th centuries for heresy.

The history of Don Luis de Carvajal and his family, will give some insight into the strange and dangerous world of New and Old Christians, crypto-Jews and the intricate and tenuous family relationships that had to be maintained under the Inquisition.

Don Luis de Carvajal was born in 1539 in Portugal into a family apparently of Old Christians. It was not until his twenties that he learned of his family's prior Jewish background. To maintain his business and social standing and to strengthen his Christian credentials, he chose to marry Dona Guiomar de Ribera of a well-known Catholic family. He shortly found that his new wife was deeply involved with the Jewish faith. He attempted to have her leave Judaism, with no success.[2] As his business was faltering, he felt that going to the New World might be a good option. He did that in a most impressive way. He petitioned King Philip II to give him a charter of a gigantic tract of land in New Spain (Mexico), which he acquired in May 1579. The territory extended from just north of Mexico City, to what is now southern Texas, and from the shores of the Gulf of

Mexico in the east, to the Gulf of California in the west.

Carvajal, a devout Catholic, was named governor of what was called the New Kingdom of Leon. He was given rights to bring in colonists at his own expense, and he brought in 100-200 families. He and his family arrived in 1580, although his wife remained behind. Carvajal was even exempted from presenting the critical "limpieza de sangre," the certificates of proof of four generations of Catholic ancestry, and Catholic blood purity. This proof had been a requirement since 1449 for Spaniards placed in key governmental posts. He and his family were believed by the Spanish to be true and faithful Catholics.

Among the many people Don Luis brought to New Spain were his sister, Donna Francisca, her husband, Don Francisco Rodriguez de Matos (who apparently was a "rabbi" in an existing crypto-Jewish group), and eight of their nine children. The ninth was a Catholic priest.

Once in Mexico, Isabel, one of Donna Francisca's daughters, tried to convince Don Luis, her uncle the governor, to practice Judaism, as she informed him that many in the family did. Isabel was told emphatically to never mention that subject again. From that point on a chain of disasters ensued. In March 1586, Isabel was arrested for practicing Judaism and was tortured by the Holy Office of the Inquisition. Her brother, Luis, two sisters, their mother and the governor, Don Luis, were put in jail.

At the governor's trial he was found guilty of harboring Judaizers and of not denouncing his sister. He was given a sentence of one year in jail and six years in exile. The cries under torture of Isabel's mother, Donna Francisca, caused her son, Luis, and other family members to confess to being crypto-Jews. They named 116 people who had come from Spain as crypto-Jews. Most of the family were, surprisingly, released after eight years, in 1594. After release, Luis maintained his Jewish faith almost openly, and he with his three sisters and mother were then rearrested and burned at the autos-da-fé of 1596, 1599 and 1601 in Mexico City, as were a great many others in the community. When Luis was killed, he declared that, "This is the path to the glory of Paradise. . .I would give away a thousand (lives), if I had them, for the faith of each of His holy commandments." Most of Carvajal's family were burned alive, their wealth, plantations and mines confiscated. Don Luis de Carvajal died during his year in jail. The huge tract of land given to Don Luis, with so much potential, was later named *The Tragic Square.*

Mexico, under Spanish/Franciscan control, was one of the most violent and aggressive areas of the Inquisition, rivaling at times the brutal occurrences in Toledo and other parts of Spain. After this attack by the Inquisition on the governor's family, many crypto-Jews escaped north into what is now southern Texas and New Mexico, probably by the 1590s, and some went to the Caribbean.

Over the next twenty-five years there were some 879 trials by the Inquisition. A large number of trials were seen in 1646, and a huge auto-da-fé took place on April 11, 1649 with 108 crypto-Jews burned alive that day.

There are some records of early Jewish entry in the southwest. Juan Gomez Barragan went into what is now the state of New Mexico in about 1615, when the area had sparse Spanish outposts. He was arrested by the Spanish for speaking Hebrew, and he died in prison. Crypto-Jews continued to drift in small numbers into the vast southwest, prior to the first group of Jews that would enter New Amsterdam in 1654. But these arrivals in the southwest seem to have been very isolated groups or individuals who were scattered over the extensive Spanish controlled territories.

THE JEWISH COLONIZATION OF THE CARIBBEAN

The few Jews who came into what eventually would be New York harbor and were met by Peter Stuyvesant in 1654 were the vanguard of a U.S. Jewish population that would eventually grow to six million. It must be noted that prior to their arrival in the American colonies, many Jews, who left Recife, Amsterdam and various European countries, established by the mid 1600s prosperous communities in the Caribbean, that included operation of sugar plantations. They were also actively engaged in international maritime trade. The earliest synagogues in the Western Hemisphere (after Recife) were erected in Guiana, Curaçao, Surinam, Barbados, St. Thomas, Jamaica and Trinidad.

In the 1600s the British, Dutch and French moved into the West Indies. By the 1650 to 1660s, Jewish settlements extended throughout the Caribbean. Caribbean Jews would serve (along with those in London and Amsterdam) as important sources of funding and encouragement, as well as a source of immigrants for the early American colonies. By the early 1700s there were significant social ties between Jewish communities on the Caribbean islands and the early American colonial settlements.

Curaçao. The Dutch captured Curaçao from Spain in 1634. The Dutch West India Company planned to use the island as a place to re-supply Dutch ships then sailing through the Caribbean, and as a base to fight regional enemies. Peter Stuyvesant was named its governor in 1642, and the island rapidly became part of the then active Dutch slave-trading network. Dutch colonists, including some Jews, came there in 1651. An agricultural settlement was established, named *De Hoop* (The Hope) by a Portuguese Jew named Joao Ilhao (or d'Illan). Additional Jews arrived from Portugal and Spain, escaping the Inquisition. In 1654 most of the Jews leaving Recife after its re-capture by the

Portuguese found their way back to Amsterdam and some to the Caribbean, while a small number eventually landed in New Amsterdam. However, by 1659 many of the Brazilian Jews who had returned to Amsterdam left again for the New World, settling in Curaçao. This westward emigration continued through the late 1600s.

The Bet Chayim cemetery was consecrated in 1659, and in the same year a Torah was sent from Amsterdam. In 1674 a building was purchased and endorsed as the first Sephardic synagogue. Other buildings were consecrated for use as synagogues in 1692 and 1703. The 1703 synagogue had some 200 seats for men and 80 for women. In 1690 about 90 Jews left Curaçao for Newport, Rhode Island, due to a local epidemic. In 1729 there was need for a larger synagogue, and Mikvé Israel was constructed on Columbusstratt replacing the 1703 synagogue. It was dedicated on the eve of Passover in 1732 and remains the oldest, and still active, synagogue in the Western Hemisphere. None of the other early synagogues in Curaçao remain.

Its floor is covered with sand as a remembrance of the 40 years of wandering of the Jewish people through the desert, as well as to evoke their ancestor's history of being secret Jews and conversos, when sand on the floor served to muffle some of the sounds of movement and worship from the ever present Inquisitional tormentors and neighborhood spies.

In the 18th century Curaçao was the largest Jewish settlement in the Western Hemisphere. By 1750 there were about 1500 Jews in Curaçao, a number that New York would not see until 1825. By 1770 Jews were 50% of the island's white population. International trade became one of the main economic engines. Additionally, some plantations grew corn and sugar, as well as various fruits and vegetables used mainly for internal consumption.

To accommodate a growing need for religious services across St. Anna Bay in Otrabanda (literally, The Other

Side), a short-lived congregation Neve Shalom (Peaceful Dwelling Place) was established in 1740, under the control of Mikvé Israel. However, its name was certainly not a predictor of its future. Neve Shalom became the focus of conflicts between strong personalities over various religious standards. Samuel Mendes de Sola, the religious leader of Mikvé Israel who had studied at Etz Haim in Amsterdam, was a lightning rod for a growing number of these conflicts. Being hot-tempered, and certain of the truth, violent arguments on the interpretation of the bible ensued. Some sermons would lead to fights breaking out in the synagogue's yard, and at times during burial services.

There were serious concerns that the cohesiveness of the entire community would be undermined. In time, through difficult and complex negotiations with the governments of both Curaçao and Amsterdam, peace was restored in the Jewish community. During one dispute in 1750 regarding the recently established Neve Shalom, the Prince of Orange-Nassau had to decree that "...all the dissenting members of the Jewish Portuguese Nation...shall again join the congregation to be governed as of old by the Parnassim and Board of the Synagogue according to the Jewish Portuguese Congregation..."[3] He also decreed that a solemn thanksgiving and prayer day be held to celebrate the end of the dispute. Both Jews and Christians attended that service, conducted by Mendes de Sola.

Mikvé Israel was known in time as the "Mother Congregation of the New World," lending aid to various synagogues including the two earliest ones built in the British colonies – Shearith Israel in New York in 1729, and the Touro synagogue in Newport, Rhode Island in 1763. The population of the island was augmented at various times by immigration from Europe when there was increased violent activity of the Inquisition. On the other hand, hurricanes, epidemics and wars involving England, France and the United States would cause rapid loss in population, particularly in the early 1800's.

In 1860 the desire for reform in the Orthodox services reached Curaçao, when some members of Mikvé Israel pressed for changes in the Sephardic Orthodox ritual. Their requests failed, and one of the very few Sephardic Orthodox Reform congregations was established – Temple Emanuel. In time, Mikvé Israel itself changed its services and installed an organ in 1866, and used it even when the congregation was following the Orthodox ritual. The two synagogues were just a few blocks apart.

The number of Jews in Curaçao decreased to a few hundred by the early 1900s. After World War II Ashkenazim from central Europe came in increasing numbers and by 1959 Congregation Shaarei Tzedek (Gates of Righteousness) was formed. In 1964 Temple Emanuel rejoined Mikvé Israel, creating Mikvé Israel-Emanuel, with the formal name of *United Netherlands Portuguese Congregation Mikvé Israel-Emanuel.* It is now associated with the Reconstructionist movement. At about this time mixed seating of the congregation was initiated. There are eighteen Torah scrolls in the Ark, (some older than the synagogue itself), with a few wound on solid silver rollers. There are four large chandeliers, each with 24 candlesticks; one of the chandeliers from the 1703 synagogue. There are now about 350 members in Mikvé Israel-Emanuel and half that number in Congregation Shaarei Tzedek. The former Temple Emanuel building remains, but has been sold.

St. Eustatius. Jews were there from about 1660, although the first active Jewish settlement is recorded about 1722. A burial ground was established by 1739, and a synagogue built in 1740. The building was 27'x40' and two stories high. The Jews in Curaçao aided in its construction. It was called *Honen Dallin* (He who is gracious to the poor). In 1760 conflicts between the Ashkenazim and Sephardim were so frequent the government had to step in to resolve and set ground rules regarding the disputes.[4] In 1772 a hurricane damaged the synagogue, and Shearith Israel in New York, as well as synagogues in Curaçao and Amsterdam, aided in its rebuilding. St. Eustatius became a major port for the trans-shipment of goods of all kind to the American patriots during the Revolutionary War – to the great consternation of the British. It is believed that by 1781 there were 400 Jews.

In February of that year the British captured the island from the Dutch, and the problems transferring private property were addressed by Edmund Burke in the British Parliament. He stated that: "Orders were given that (the Jews) should be stripped, and all the linings of their clothes ripped-up, that every shilling of money which they might attempt to conceal and carry off should be discovered and taken from them. . ."[5] And later he noted that other inhabitants (such as the French and Dutch) could depart peacefully. The French captured the island in November 1781, the Dutch regained control in 1784. But the Jewish population slowly dwindled from that time on. Some of the external walls of the original synagogue can still be seen.

St. Thomas, U.S. Virgin Islands. This island was settled very early in the 16th century. Sugar plantations were established by Jews escaping from Portugal, who imported sugar cane from Madeira to establish large plantations. Sugar mills were built, and a most significant sugar export trade was established. By 1550 production of the 60 plantations was 3.75 million pounds.[6] Additional Jews came after the Recife expulsions. Congregation Bracha v'Shalom Vegemiluth Hasadim (Blessing, Peace and Loving Deeds) was established in 1796, although there were small, earlier Jewish communities. At present this congregation's 1833 building in Charlotte Amalie has about 80 families, with some 300 Jews in St. Thomas. The synagogue still maintains a sand floor.

Barbados. The first Jews came in the late 1620's. Sugar production was being developed by 1640 as a replacement for cotton and tobacco (considered to be of poor quality). In 1654 Jews came to Barbados from Recife, Brazil following its recapture by the Portuguese. The techniques of efficient sugar production were brought to the island by these new colonists. The dramatic increase in sugar production over the Caribbean basin would actually result in the lowering of world sugar prices and would have a significant impact on the Brazilian sugar-based economy.[7]

A synagogue, Shaare Tzedek (Gates of Justice), was built in 1654, and in 1657 they received a Torah scroll from Amsterdam. Barbados was the first English territory to accept Jews since the expulsion of Jews from England in 1290. But over time, restrictions on Jews employing Christians resulted in the Jews being involved to a greater extent in sugar trading rather than in the actual agricultural production of sugar. Jews were involved with tobacco crops as well. In 1660 a visitor to Barbados stated that the Jews "do so swarm" on the island, and by 1672 a Calendar of State Papers noted that Jews were "against all Christians and . . .are dangerous, inhuman and dangerous to Barbadian security."[8] New arrivals from Brazil established the first modern sugar mills. Petitions and other writings against Jews increased; special additional taxes, in pounds of sugar, were assessed on them for items such as "ye repiring the highway." Despite these ongoing problems, another synagogue, Nidhei Israel (Exiles of Israel), was built in 1717. By 1750 there were some 400-500 Jews – about 3% of the population.

Jews were to be found in almost every British colony in the 17th and 18th centuries, including Barbadian Jews in the colonial cities of Newport, Philadelphia and Charleston. Their success in Barbados made them despised within the island. P.F. Campbell, a Barbadian historian, wrote that the Jews were intensely disliked as they "were shrewd businessmen and drove a hard bargain," and until the 19th century they were subject to special civil penalties. Their numbers dwindled and by the beginning of the 20th century Jewry was hardly represented in the island.

The 1654 synagogue was destroyed by the 1831 hurricane. Rebuilt in 1833, it seriously deteriorated and was sold in 1929. The building was bought back in 1983 and Nidhe Israel was restored. An adjacent cemetery contains legible engravings on the tombstones going back to at least the 1660s. There are now just sixteen Jewish families on the island.

Jamaica. The Spanish settled in Jamaica in 1509. Brazilian Jewish refugees came to Jamaica when the Spanish lost the island to the British in 1655. By 1670 there were many sugar mills in operation by Jews who also were involved in coffee-growing, and the export of ginger, indigo and cocoa. And in the same year the British were actively seeking Jewish immigrants to emigrate to Jamaica. At the same time there were serious attempts by English merchants to take away the economic rights granted to the Jews because they were effectively competing with the Christian business community.

The governor stated in 1689 that liberty of conscience can be given "to all person except papists." Further, he felt that the King could not have more useful subjects than the Jews. But Christian merchants wanting the Jews expelled took the position that "the Jews eat us and our children out of all trade. . .had we not had warning from other colonies, we should see our streets and ships crowded with them. This means taking our children's bread and giving it to the Jews."[9]

In 1724 the British trading entities denounced Jewish competition as ruinous, and advocates within the Christian planters pressed for expulsion of the Jews. Additionally, there were ongoing claims that Jews were disloyal and plotting nefarious deeds with the slave population. The legislature imposed a special tax on Jews and made them collect the tax from their own communities. By 1740 the fight for more equality by the Jews seemed to have been won. About 900 Jews were then in Jamaica. An ordained rabbi was on the island by 1760, far ahead of any in the colonies. The early synagogues were Nevey Shalom, Beit Yaacob and Sharei Hashamayim (Gates of Heaven), the same name as the Bevis Marks synagogue in London. Sharei Hashamayim remained from 1774 to 1883. The present synagogue is the United Congregation of Israelites Sharei Shalom (Gates of Peace) in Kingston. Like the synagogues in St. Thomas, the floor is covered with sand.

Surinam (Dutch Guiana). Jewish settlements occurred by 1639. At that time Surinam was a British colony. The English stated "we have found that the Hebrew Nation is Proved of utility and Blessing for the colonies." The Jews thrown out of Recife, Brazil by the Portuguese and out of Cayenne by the French, turned parts of Surinam (northeastern South America) into a healthy economic enterprise. In 1665 a British grant of safety was given to the Jews in Surinam, the first such agreement between Britain and Jews. This promise of safety was probably tied to the colony's need for sugar production, as well as the governments dire need for immigrants. In 1685 (after the Dutch received Surinam in "trade" for the land that would be Manhattan Island) Beracha v'Shalom was built. By 1694 there were 92 Sephardic families, a dozen Ashkenazi families and fifty single individuals of unknown Jewish association. Surinam then had at least one Ashkenazi and one Sephardic synagogue. And as happened in St. Eustatius, the two Jewish communities were in social conflict, and not mutually supporting each other. Some remains of Beracha v'Shalom still exist, and apparently two synagogues remain in use in Paramaribo.

There were additional Jewish communities in Trinidad-Tobago, Nevis (synagogue and cemetery by 1688), Antigua, St. Kitts, Martinique and Guadaloupe. Complex trading networks were developed throughout the Caribbean with Amsterdam, London, Surinam, Africa and later on with the early American colonies, and even with Spanish-held areas using appropriate commercial middlemen. Curaçao and Barbados became major hubs of international trade. It was a truly amazing and dynamic period, but there were always attempts to limit the rights of Jews, particularly when Christian merchants felt that their own prosperity was being impacted by these active newcomers.

So enterprising were these new residents that a note was received by the Dutch West India Co. in 1684 that: "The Jew Salomon de la Roche having died some eight or nine months ago. . .the trade in vanilla has come to an end, since no one here knows how to prepare it so as to develop the proper aroma and keep it from spoiling."[10] The mobility and accomplishments of the Jews in the Caribbean during the 17th and 18th centuries is truly a source of amazement to this day.

The trading networks that evolved with the Caribbean islands led to close economic and social ties with many of the American colonies – and in particular with Newport, New York and Charleston. The Caribbean would be the place of origin of some of the earliest settlers and traders now moving to the American colonies.

The Jews had moved to the New World through South America, Mexico and the Caribbean. But what of the ever-present Inquisition which followed them from the Old World? It was still in business and active in many places. In the best of circumstances religious and ethnic hatreds die exceedingly slowly.

5

THE LONG ROAD TO RELIGIOUS TOLERANCE AND CIVIC EQUALITY

Before discussing the early congregations in the colonies, it would be useful to get a sense of the environment, both religious and civic, that the early Jews faced. Religious and civic equality was still far in the future for the great majority of the Jews entering America. Most of the colonies operated with "state" religions defined in their code of laws, supported through the general tax base. Even in the most tolerant, the Carolina colony, the Anglican church and later both the clergy and the maintenance of the churches, were supported by the government. And of course, the laws on voting and serving in the legislatures throughout the colonies were a varied list of barriers affecting Jews, but also in some cases affecting Catholics and various branches of Protestantism.

Despite what many have heard about the search for religious freedom in the colonies, it was selective religious freedom – for my religion and not necessarily yours. True religious tolerance from governmental entities was in very short supply.

There is a tale of two ministers discussing differences in their creeds. It was a beautiful lesson in tolerance which one minister summed up by saying, "Yes, we both worship the same God, you in your way and I in His."

Although a light story, it revealed that there were differences everywhere that some took (and still take!) very, very seriously. In some cases the colonies were intolerant, in that various forms of Protestantism were highly antagonistic to one another, and of course Protestantism vs. Catholicism was a continuing battle in the colonies. There were instances where oaths for citizenship or public office were modified and phrases dropped to accommodate "other" religions. In fact, many of the religious based restrictions in state laws and state constitutions lasted for long periods of time after the adoption of the U.S. Constitution and Bill of Rights.

Some of the apparent acceptance of Jews in selected colonies could have been due to the small number present. And they were generally (albeit not always) accepted as active and industrious colonizers supporting the local economy. Their numbers were small – only about 1,500-2,000 out of 3.9 million in the general population during the Revolutionary War. The main Christian religions were busy with their continuing, long-standing, well-honed disputes carried over from Europe. Some animosity toward Jews could have been truly driven by religious beliefs, but it seems that some may have been happening (or deftly used) as a means of trying to clear the field from competition both in commerce and politics.

However, the religious animosity was not in the same league in its tenacity or in the aggressive punishment for those of the "wrong" faith as compared to Europe. The matches, stakes and bayonets were left in the Old World. There was little bloodshed or taking of life here. Restrictions on allowing Jews to vote or hold office had a long life, well into the 19th century in some states. There were a large number of attempts to keep legislatures Protestant, and exclude Jews. Only one state, New York, granted complete equality in 1777 to Jews, but not to Catholics or atheists, among others. The constitutions of the states at the end of the Revolutionary War excluded Jews from civic equality, and it was a very long time before some state constitutions were modified.

Examples of religious based intolerance and the slow march towards civic and political equality are many.

Only a few such examples will be noted to give a sense of the times during which the initial congregations and synagogues were built. It is of interest that the colonies apparently never brought out the militia to enforce religious doctrine. The fact that there were so many dissenters of various types reduced the power of those bent on instituting some form of theocracy. Clearly dissenters (including Jews) took the attitude that, "We've lived through worse, and I can operate within the system to do what I want." They were intent on building their social and business lives and saw these political and religious obstacles as bumps in the road to be avoided, or to be worked around. If truly bothersome, there were always the adjacent colonies that may have had greater opportunities or an easier road.

In Massachusetts in the early days of the colony there was an attempt to impose religious uniformity through compulsory church attendance, fines for absence from services, and compulsory taxes to support the parish church. These desires for forced uniformity in religion were similar to those seen in many European countries from which they came. Some 35 churches were formed by 1640, twenty years after the arrival of the Mayflower. The Puritans believed that a person was wholly sinful and in need of severe discipline to ensure one was on the correct path. The Puritans had a very positive and deeply held religious affinity towards the Old Testament, but to have Jews in the colony not practicing the Puritan's local religion was another thing. Puritans desired a godly community where their church and state were one and the same. Troublemakers were dealt with publically and expeditiously.

Rev. Rodger Williams, however, felt that the Puritan clergy impacted the freedom he believed belonged to individual congregations. He also felt that the Puritan clergy had acquired for themselves great political and civil control that actually thwarted the desires of the congregations. Actually, one of the original concerns of the Puritan movement as it started in England in the 1560s was that the religious establishment of Elizabeth I was too political and too controlling. Williams did not like the settler's acquisition of Indian lands. For these thoughts he was banished in Oct. 1635 to Rhode Island. It was also a crime for shipmasters to bring Quakers to Massachusetts, and by 1658 the banished Quakers were subject to the death penalty if they returned. Edward Wilson, former governor of New Plymouth, felt that the punishment of Quakers (such as lashes with a tarred rope) was the will of Jehovah.[1] The Puritans desired religious freedom for themselves, but certainly not for others. True liberty of conscience would have destroyed their movement.

In 1666 the colony charter stated that the Christian faith "is the only end of this plantation and over this plantation." The Puritans felt that their goal was to achieve a godly community, where church and state were one. John Cotton declared in Massachusetts, "Democracy -- I do not conceive that God did ever ordain it as a fit government for either church or Commonwealth."[2] Increase Mather decried the "hideous clamor for liberty of conscience," and utterly abhorred tolerance of religion for man. Cotton Mather and others believed that Jews were to be won to Christianity through the Old Testament by showing them that the prophecies all pointed to Jesus as the Messiah. If the Jews could be brought over, then the coming of Jesus was imminent. But over time, with the decrease in Puritan domination and the pressure of commercial growth, the ability of the clergy to keep the population in their religious box waned. There was less attention to one John Maylem, in furthering the creed, who sang on the Sabbath:

> Henceforth let none, in peril of their lives,
> Attempt a journey, or embrace their wives.

The younger people would not be bound by these narrow religious precepts. Things did change over time. By 1687 Anglican services were held in Boston. By 1720, Isaac Lopez, a Jew, was elected constable in Boston.[3]

Rhode Island, under Roger Williams, offered a democratic refuge from religious prosecution. He was banished from Puritan Massachusetts due to his religious beliefs and political and social ideas. And he established a colony that was unique in allowing religious tolerance which brought people into the colony from both England and Massachusetts. By 1663 a grant of liberty of conscience was established by royal charter.

Neverthless, as local people in power changed their position, original laws allowing freedom of religion were amended in 1715. The laws now excluded Jews and Catholics from the rights of citizenship, and the formal religion of the colony was for all intents and purposes Protestantism.[4] As Massachusetts became more tolerant, Rhode Island, became much more restrictive and intolerant. It took some 127 additional years, until 1842, for both religious and civic equality to be regained. Rhode Island's haven for dissidents was unfortunately short-lived. Jews who could not get citizenship in Rhode Island moved to more tolerant Massachusetts, where it was available. A complete reversal!

In 1639 there was a vote in Connecticut stating that "the Scriptures doe holde forth a perfect role for the direction and government of all men in all duties." Congregationalism was the state religion from about 1662 to 1818. With the end of the state religion, Jews were the first to be given the rights of the rest of the citizens to vote or hold public office. In 1843 they were allowed to practice their religion openly, but the resources were lacking to build a synagogue. Judah Touro of New Orleans (son of Isaac Touro, the former religious leader in Newport) gave a bequest in 1856 that allowed the building of Connecticut's first synagogue (Beth Israel) in Hartford.[5]

The colony of Maryland was founded in 1632 under a grant of land given to George Calvert (Lord Baltimore) by King Charles I. Calvert wanted the colony to be a haven for persecuted Catholics, and by 1649 a "Toleration Act" was passed granting freedom to all Christians. The tolerant times would not last, unfortunately. Both Catholics, Protestants, and Puritans came to the colony, and disputes gradually became severe. With increasing Protestant numbers they gained control in 1654, and Roman Catholics were thrown out of the legislature. One part of the Toleration Act addressed any speech or action "that blasphemes God, or deny our Savior Jesus Christ to be the sonne of God or shall deny the Holy Trinity. . .shall be punished with death and confiscation. . .of his or her lands and goods to the Lord Proprietary and his heires." The penalty for blasphemy was death, but it was reduced to an "admonishment" by 1654.

By 1656, with Lord Calvert back in power, the "admonishment" was thrown out and the death penalty reinstituted. This was just in time for a Jewish physician, Jacob Lumbrozo, to be charged in 1658 with making improper comments in a discussion with others regarding Christ and the resurrection. He was charged with blasphemy. There was testimony against him, but, luckily (since he admitted and made light of his "blasphemy" on the stand), an amnesty period had gone into effect in honor of Richard Cromwell (son of Oliver). His case was declared over and apparently no one else was ever charged.[6] In time, even in early Maryland, things changed. Lumbrozo remained in the colony, became a citizen in 1663, imported servants, became a country squire, and when he died, left most of his estate to his wife, and 4,000 pounds of tobacco to his sister, Rivka, in Holland. Quite a turnaround! However, Dr. Lumbrozo would have had to be around for some 160 more years to gain full civic equality. In 1692 Maryland became a Royal colony and established the Episcopalian religion as its "state" religion.

It wasn't until 1825 that a *Jew Bill* (its formal legislative title!) was passed in Maryland, by a majority of one, that allowed Jews to hold office without taking an oath professing Christian belief.[7] A reconfirming vote passed in 1826, after one defeat. The Jew Bill Act was first submitted to the legislature in 1818. Its purpose was: "To consider the justice and expediency of extending to those persons professing the Jewish religion the same privileges that are enjoyed by Christians." Before passing it, the Act was discussed for 8 years. One of the authors of the bill was Thomas Kennedy, a non-Jew in the legislature. It was demeaned as "Kennedy's Jew Baby." Kennedy stated that if "Christianity cannot stand without the aid of persecution . . .let it fall!"

It is easy to assume the legislatures' hearts were really not in it. *Now this was only some 40 years after our Federal Constitution and Bill of Rights called for no religious requirements for holding public office.*

There were many continuing attempts to keep legislatures Protestant (for example, New Jersey in 1776), or if not that, at least Christian. There were attempts to expunge the Federal laws that said there would be no religious barriers for voting or holding office, and many colonies required various Christological oaths.

The Virginia colonial assembly passed a law in 1696 "whereby the glory of God may be advanced, the Church (of England) propagated and the people edified." Salaries for ministers were set at 16,000 pounds of tobacco per year, which continued until the Revolutionary War. (Whether there was a cost of living adjustment is not known.) In 1755 a crop failure resulted in altering payment to money.

Until the Revolutionary War, Jews in Virginia would have to take an oath "upon the true faith of a Christian" (which would keep out Jews), and would also have to swear that the sacrament of the Lord's Supper did not involve transubstantiation (which a Jew could agree on), but which would keep out Catholics.[8] Religious complications were lying everywhere!

The Anglican church in Virginia was the only legal religion. Jews, for example, were not allowed to legally perform marriages. Additionally, no non-Christian or Catholic or black could testify or be a witness in colonial Virginia courts. This also prevented certain groups, such as Jews, from using the court system for their own grievances or getting restitution. A 1735 law forbid Jews from having Christian servants.

A bill supported by Thomas Jefferson in 1786 established general religious freedom. An attempt was made to amend the bill by inserting "Almighty God Jesus Christ, the author of our religion." It failed. Yet, a 1792 bill was formally enacted that again revoked religious liberty and imposed the Christian faith on the population. It was finally rescinded in 1802.

Some acts that would appear to be solely against Jews were, in fact, likely targeting Catholics, who were higher on the list of perceived "problems" for some colonies. While civic equality had not been fully achieved, Jews started to receive some Federal appointments, such as four ambassadorships between 1810-1820, and Gershom Mendes Seixas of Shearith Israel in New York became a trustee of Columbia College (forerunner of Columbia University) from 1784 to 1815.

Although the issues of tolerance in South Carolina will be addressed separately in Chapter 7, one note should be mentioned here. There was the continuing annoying issue of Blue Laws in the South Carolina colony in 1882 and in other places in different times that affected Jewish merchants who wished to close on Saturday, but reopen on Sunday. South Carolina, seeing that there was a problem, must have carefully studied the issue, for they finally repealed the Blue Laws in 1983.[9]

Other colonies were addressing the same issue of the "profanation of the Lord's Day." In the early 1600s Virginia had a Sunday law that made attendance at religious services compulsory. The third offense was apparently punishable by death. Many of the early colonies had similar laws without such dramatic conclusions. In 1695 New York had a law against desecrating "The Lord's Day." This Sunday Law was rescinded after the Revolutionary War. A subsequent attempt to reinstitute the Sunday restrictions failed, but in 1788 an "Act for Supressing Immorality" was approved. It read in part: *"It is hereby enacted. . .that there shall be no traveling, service labor or working. . .shooting, sporting, playing, horse racing or frequenting tippling-houses. . .on the first day of the week, commonly called Sunday."* Goods found to be on sale could be forfeited and contributed to the poor.

There were attempts to defeat the act based on both its detriment to non-Christians and the claim that the act was "repugnant to the Constitution." Speeches by legislators noted that *"Sabbath breaking is an offense against God and religion. . .in a country professing Christianity, and the corruption of morals that usually follows its profanation."* Also, *"Every man was left to worship the Almighty in the way that pleased him, and he might keep what day he pleased; but if he does not chuse (sic) to keep the Sabbath, do not let him disturb them that do."*

On the other side of the issue it was said that *"a Jew, to be consistent, is obliged to keep holy the 7th day of the week, which is Saturday, and to prohibit him from working on a Sunday would be taxing him one sixth part of his time. This was not equal liberty, one of the boasted blessings of our government."* The Sunday law passed 34 to 5.[10]

Many of the original states retained the basic laws, and constitutions that were in effect while they were colonies. Some states during the post-Revolutionary War period actually changed from supporting a single branch of a Christian religion to supporting multiple branches of Christianity. It was looked on as a form of equality – no longer supporting, for example, solely the Anglican church, but rather Christianity in general. As William Tennent put it in 1778 as he addressed the South Carolina legislature, it *"opens the door to equal incorporations of all denominations"* where *"Christianity is the established religion of the State."*

But other states were moving in different directions. New York in 1777 was the first to abolish from its constitution most religious preferences, excepting Catholics. South Carolina changed its constitution in 1790, giving equal freedom to Protestants, Catholics and Jews. On the same day, February 19, 1791, both Kahal Kadosh Beth Elohim and St. Mary's Roman Catholic church (across the street from each other) were incorporated under the new state constitution granting free exercise of religion. Virginia and Rhode Island had complete religious freedom after the revolution. It took many years for other states to review and change their constitutions and remove religious-oriented sections. Religious qualifications for office were eliminated in Pennsylvania and South Carolina in 1790; Delaware in 1792; Georgia in 1798; Connecticut in 1818; Massachusetts in 1821, and Maryland in 1826.

New Hampshire was most restrictive in retaining rights for Protestants and held them the longest. No one could be elected to the state legislature, House or Senate, or be Governor, unless Protestant, and had to have a designated minimum amount of land holdings. The exclusion of Catholics and Jews remained until 1876. A clause in the constitution would allow towns (if they wished) to tax all citizens for the support of Protestant teachers of religion (basically it was said, to teach morality). There clearly was a high degree of "concern" about the Catholics in the Anglican colonies. The general ban or restriction on Catholics was a remnant of the battle for control of the monarchy between Protestantism and Catholicism in England,, when Pope Clement VIII would not annul the marriage between Henry VIII and Katharine of Aragon.

New Hampshire waited until 1868 to remove a Christian oath as a requirement for public office. Eventually, the state decided to change the word "Protestant" that still remained in its constitution to a more encompassing but still restrictive word, "Christian."[11] But in the early part of the 20th century it was made clear that New Hampshire voters would not go any further at that time, as they turned down a referendum that would delete the word "Christian" from their constitution, which would have resulted in encompassing all beliefs (or non-beliefs) held by their citizens.

During this rather lengthy period of revision of laws and constitutions, some states actually allowed broader religious freedoms, even if it conflicted with the formal words in their constitutions. But we know that intolerance was not just against Jews, Catholics and various branches of Protestantism. There was, of course, the major festering issue of slavery, which was endemic to some of the colonies and was a major consideration throughout the Caribbean and South America. We should keep in mind that slavery was key to the agricultural economy of the New World from the 1500s on. There were major trading routes between Africa, the American colonies, and the Caribbean supporting the transportation and the sale of African, Caribbean and South American native people into slavery. This issue would at a later date divide and rack this country. The reverberations of the slavery issue is still with us; slavery still exists in various forms in many parts of the world.

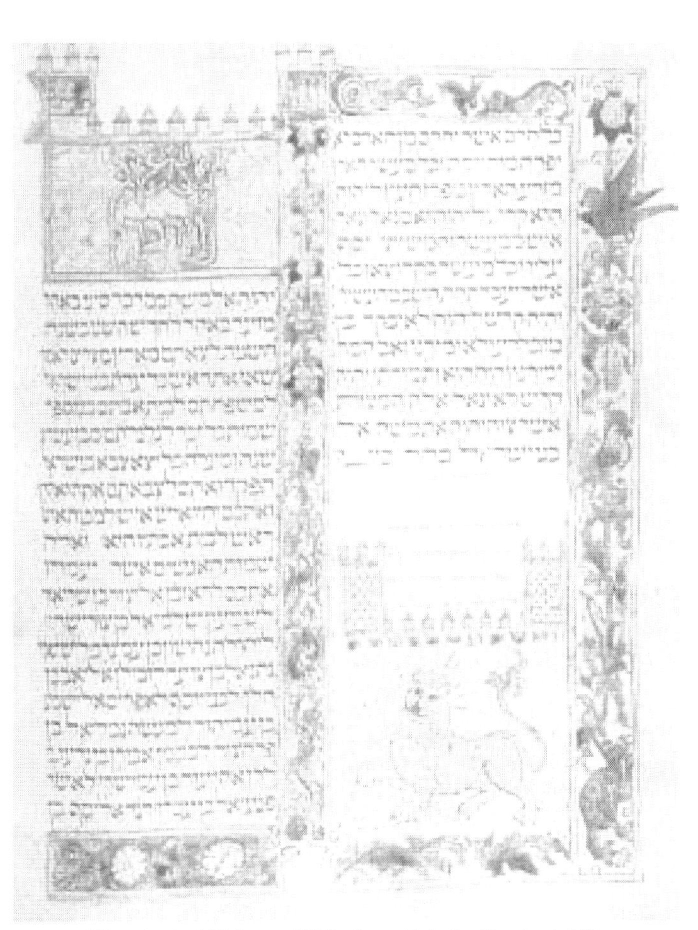

Illuminated Hebrew Bible from Toledo, Spain, 1491.
Courtesy the Hispanic Society of America, NY

The spread of the anti-Jewish riots in 1391.
From A Historical Atlas of the Jewish People © by Eli Barnavi © 1992 Hatchette Literature. Permission of Schoken Books, division of Random House, Inc.

Menasseh Ben Israel (etching by Rembrandt van Rijn). Important figure in helping Jews return to Great Britain in the 17th Century after being expelled in 1290.

Isaac Aboab de Fonseca, the first rabbi in theWestern Hemisphere; came from Holland to Recife, Brazil in 1642.
Courtesy of the American Jewish Historical Society, Newton Center, MA and New York, NY

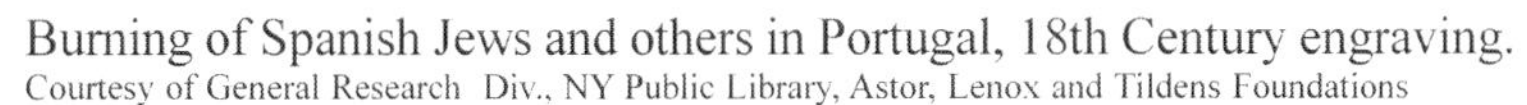

Burning of Spanish Jews and others in Portugal, 18th Century engraving.
Courtesy of General Research Div., NY Public Library, Astor, Lenox and Tildens Foundations

Mikvé Israel-Emanuel, Curaçao
Author's photograph

18th century engraving by I. M. Belisario of 1701 Bevis Marks Synagogue
Courtesy of New York Public Library, Dorot Jewish Division; Astor, Lenox and Tilden Foundations.

The Ark of the Bevis Marks Synagogue, London.
Courtesy of the American Jewish Archives, Cincinnati, Ohio

Interior of Mikvé Israel-Emanuel, Curaçao
Courtesy of the American Jewish Archives, Cincinnati, Ohio

Interior of Bracha v'Shalom Vegemiluth Hasadim, Charlotte Amalie, St. Thomas, U.S. Virgin Islands
Courtesy of the American Jewish Archives, Cincinnati, Ohio

Interior of Nidhe Israel, Barbados
Author's photograph

Exterior of former Temple Emanuel, Curaçao. The congregation joined Mikvé Israel in 1964. The building has been sold.
Courtesy of the American Jewish Archives, Cincinnati, Ohio

A REVIEW OF THE FIVE EARLIEST COLONIAL JEWISH COMMUNITIES

6A

FIRST JEWS INTO AMERICA, DUTCH NEW AMSTERDAM AND PETER STUYVESANT

While anchored in Lower New York Bay in 1524, Giovanni da Verrazano remarked that the area is "not without some properties of value," and noted its "commodiousness and beauty." This was quite a prescient statement for 1524.

As far as it is known today Joseph (Joachim) Gaunse (or Ganz) from Prague, would be, in 1585, the first Jew to set foot on the east coast of the United States. And, as noted earlier, at nearly the same time a very few Sephardim would be entering Texas and Arizona from Mexico. Gaunse, educated as a metallurgist and mining engineer, was brought to England in 1581 by Sir Walter Raleigh and the Royal Mining Company who were planning the first colonization of the east coast.

At that time Jews were still banned from England, but Gaunse had developed a special expertise in more rapidly smelting copper, a capability that was needed to support the continuing conflict between England (Queen Elizabeth I) and Spain. Gaunse was a "mynerall man," one of 110 people (including a mathematician) on the first attempted colonization of Roanoke Island in Pamlico Sound, North Carolina, near Nags Head in 1585. Gaunse sought silver, copper and "many sortes of apothecorie drugs."[1] If proper ore was found it would be used to improve the casting of guns against the Spanish Armada. What was mainly found was sand and pebbles and kaolin. The latter is a form of clay that was probably used by the small British group to stop diarrhea, but I'm not sure that was what the Queen had in mind.

The British contingent had endless problems: the inability to grow timely crops to abate their hunger; having to rely on the Indians for food; poor fishing in the Sound, and disease. The Indians were not their main problem at first. In fact, some of the Indians taught the English proper fishing techniques required in the Sound's shallow waters, but the colonists were not really successful. The friendly Indians, at the same time, were rapidly falling ill and dying of European diseases (probably small pox and measles), against which the Indians had no natural immunity. Some Indians believed the English could "slae... without weapons, and not come near them." (The same rampant illnesses occurred when Columbus landed in the Caribbean, with the native Arawak Indians being nearly wiped out by diseases carried by the Spanish.)

Over time the English dependency on the Indians created hostility. The English were not prepared to live off the land and the supply ship from the mother country had not arrived. Some of the upper-class barely lifted a finger, looking to others to work for them. The entire expedition was rescued by the ever-present Sir Francis Drake, who, after decimating Hispaniola and St. Augustine, appeared off shore in June 1586 and returned Gaunse and other members to Portsmouth.

The British would attempt another landing, and finally, they established Jamestown, a colony that barely succeeded. But Roanoke Island, plus Drake's aggressiveness (plus the efforts of Sir Richard Grenville, another adventurous sea captain) clearly demonstrated to the Spanish that despite Columbus' travels, Spain would not have free reign of Western Hemisphere lands nor its trade routes. This would prove of importance to the Jews as the attempted domination by the Spanish in the New World would be under continual contention by both the British and the Dutch.

Gaunse returned to England, supporting himself

by giving Hebrew lessons. Three years later he was accussued by a Reverend Curteys of denying the divinity of Jesus Christ. The penalty was death if found guilty. During a hearing on September 15, 1589 in Bristol, England, Curteys testified that:

> "...in the howse of Mr. Richard Mayes (inn-keeper). ..Joachim (Gaunse) came into our companye unto whom I, the said Richard Curteys, spake in the Hebrew tounge to this effect: that Jesus of Nazareth, the Kinge of the Jewes, whome the Jewes crucified was and is the sonne of God. At which tyme he answered me in the Hebrew tounge; he is not the sonne of God, whose replie being so odious I spake in the English tounge to the ende that others, being there present, might hear it and witness his speeche: What, do thou denie Jesus Christ to be the sonne of God? At which tyme he answered: What needeth the almightie God to have a sonne, is he not almyghtie?"[2]

Gaunse was charged with blasphemy and with being an infidel; the case was sent from the Bristol court to the Queens Privy Council. Unfortunately, no record of what the Council did has been found. Suffice to say, the first Jew to be in the colonies (as best we know) was called to help England and its earliest colony, but, upon his return to the Mother Country was quickly enmeshed in the ongoing religious conflicts.

THE FIRST JEWS INTO DUTCH NEW AMSTERDAM

In 1621 the Dutch occupied what would be lower Manhattan with a Dutch trading post and founded New Amsterdam in 1625. And in 1626 the famous "$24 trinket transaction" with Peter Minuit and the Indians took place. The only record of the purchase is found in a letter of November 5, 1626 by Pieter Jansen, written in Amsterdam to the

States-General in The Hague.

The original is in the General Government Archives, The Hague. It reads, in part, as translated:

> "High Mighty Sirs:
> Here arrived yesterday the ship The Arms of Amsterdam which sailed from New Netherlands . . .on September 23: they report that our people are of good courage, and live peaceably. Their women, also, have borne children there, they have bought the island Manhattes (sic) from the wild men for the value of sixty guilders. . .They sowed all their grain in the middle of May, and harvested it in the middle of August. . .Herewith be ye High Mighty Sirs, commended to the Almighty's grace . . ."[3]

There was not a great movement of Dutch people from the city of Amsterdam to New Amsterdam; few in Europe saw the need to go from a comfortable, beautiful city to the edge of the wilderness. However, by 1630 there was some expansion to the "suburbs" of Breukelen and The Broncks (named after Jonas Bronck, a farmer in this northern area of the colony).

To try to bring some degree of uniformity to the community, a law was passed in 1640 that prohibited public worship of faiths other than Dutch Reform. The clear desire was to prevent the establishment of the Lutheran church. The States-General government's office in The Hague sent the following instructions to the Dutch West India Company in New Netherlands:

> "They (the colonists) shall within the territory hold no other services than that of the (Protestant Dutch) Reformed Religion in the manner in which they are at present conducted in this country and thus by their Christian life and conduct try to lead the Indians and other blind persons to the knowledge of God and His word without persecuting

> anyone on account of his faith but leaving everyone free of conscience."[4]

Starting in 1649, five years before the arrival of the Jews, the colony was governed by the very straight-laced conservative Peter Stuyvesant, who would have been happy with a simple, single religion, the Dutch Reformed Church. New Amsterdam already had a highly diverse mixture of Dutch, Danes, Swedes, Finns, Portuguese, Spaniards, Italians and others. In general, New Amsterdam was a tough town filled with traders and sailors spending their hard-earned money in beer halls before resuming their lives on the edge of the known world. The town had over 1,000 residents from some dozen countries, and probably the same number of religious beliefs. A local reported 18 languages in use.

The Dutch were close to a minority in their own colony; non-Dutch whites were nearly 50% of the population. One tenth of the population were African slaves, and some were granted "half freedom," which allowed them to marry, to move within the colony, and to own and lease property in return for annual payments in grain and furs.

In July 1654 a Jew, Jacob Barsimon, came to New Amsterdam in the ship, *Peachtree*.[5] To add to Stuyvesant's concerns twenty-three other Jewish settlers came upon the scene in September 1654 looking for refuge after a most horrendous voyage from Recife, Brazil. These early voyagers were to have a place in history as the forerunners of the future Jewish settlement and immigration to the United States. Their original destination from Recife was probably Amsterdam. The 23 Jews were waylaid and robbed by Spanish pirates, forced to change to a French ship and then arrived in New Amsterdam.[6] They lost most of their possessions during the four-month voyage and owed passage money to the ship's captain.

Governor Stuyvesant saw their arrival as a significant problem. There were two main issues. The newcomers were destitute, and Stuyvesant believed that the Jews would be a drain on the resources of the colony. The captain of the *St. Catarina* (or *St. Charles*), which brought these twenty-three Jews to North America, went to court to try to recover the cost of passage that they could not pay. To satisfy the requested payment, whatever furniture the Jews had onboard was sold by auction. Not fully covering the costs, three people were sent to debtors prison, but the shipmaster relented after awhile (probably knowing he wasn't going to get the money anyway), and they were released. The second and more critical issue was the fact that Stuyvesant wanted to be rid of the Jews, and ship them out of the colony. The interaction between Stuyvesant, the Jews and the Dutch West India Company is an intriguing chapter of Jewish immigration to the New World.

The new settlers to New Amsterdam from Brazil had been welcomed in a most egregious manner by Governor Peter Stuyvesant. Stuyvesant was a staunch Calvinist, a rigid autocratic leader, a former governor of Curaçao and was highly intolerant of religious dissenters. He was an equal-opportunity bigot and disliked all dissenters from Calvinism, with a particular dislike of Quakers and he wasn't overjoyed about Jews either. Governor Stuyvesant (one of whose titles was director-general) was very open about his autocratic manner of governing, stating that he would "govern you as a father his children."

On arriving from Amsterdam in 1647 he set up a nine-member advisory board, which he believed he could control. However, when in 1651 the advisory board asked that their grievances be sent to the Dutch home government, Stuyvesant quickly abolished the board. But this action caused the Dutch West India Company to form a municipal government in 1653 that would be more responsive to the people of New Amsterdam, and this certainly was of great annoyance to the autocratic Stuyvesant. (The Dutch West India Company had established New Amsterdam; Stuyvesant was their employee.)

His reaction upon seeing the twenty-three Jews was to refuse them entry. But rather than just throw them out, as he probably would have done earlier, he proceeded to inform his company in Amsterdam of his displeasure with the Jews. Stuyvesant had other concerns on his mind regarding the Jews, and he most ardently let the company know his feelings without mincing any words. He wrote in a letter to the Amsterdam Chamber of Directors on September 22, 1654:

> "The Jews who have arrived would nearly all like to remain here, but learning that they (with their customary usury and deceitful trading with the Christians) were very repugnant to the inferior magistrates. . .(the fact that they had been captured and robbed by privateers or pirates) they might become a charge in the coming winter, we have, for the benefit of this waek (sic) and newly developing place. . .deemed it useful to require them in a friendly way to depart; praying also most seriously in this connection. . .that the deceitful race – such hateful enemies and blasphemers of the name of Christ – be not allowed further to infect and trouble this new colony to the detraction . . .of your worships and the dissatisfaction of your worships most affectionate subjects."[7]

Stuyvesant felt it would create confusion if the Jews came to settle here, and believed that they will utilize "their customary usury and deceitful trading" with the Christians and want to build a synagogue and insist on the free and public exercise of their "abominable" religion. There was high concern that they would enter and compete with existing commercial enterprises such as the lucrative pelt trade with the Indians on the Hudson River as far north as Ft. Orange (Albany, New York), and on the South River (now the Delaware River).

When the response from Amsterdam arrived in April 26, 1655 , it told a highly disgruntled Stuyvesant that he was to let the Jews stay. The letter stated that it would be "unreasonable and unfair especially because of the considerable loss sustained by the nation, with others, in the taking of Brazil," to refuse asylum to those that had played such an important role in the Dutch Brazilian colony. And that, "After close consultation, and in consideration of the petition of the Portuguese Jews (in Amsterdam), we have determined to grant them the privilege to ply the waters of New Netherlands, to engage in trade everywhere, and to settle in all places, with the one reservation that those without funds among them are not to become burdens upon the Company or the Christian community, but are to be supported by members of their own race."[8]

The letter continued: "You may therefor shut your eyes, at least not force people's consciences, but allow everyone to have his own belief, as long as he behaves quietly and legally." The Jews could also hold religious services in private, and while they could build houses anywhere, it was suggested that they be "close together." The reply from Amsterdam probably surprised Stuyvesant, inasmuch as just four years earlier the Dutch West India Company directors wrote Stuyvesant about some Jews entering Curaçao, and stated that the Jews were.. . . "generally treacherous people in whom, therefore, not too much confidence must be placed." Another earlier note stated:

> "We cannot trust any of that nation (Jews) residing under our jurisdiction. Their immigrating and having favor granted to them must therefore be restricted henceforth that we may not nourish serpents in our bosom, who finally might devour our hearts."

The Dutch West India Company now had a far more open philosophy than Stuyvesant, feeling that almost any immigrant willing to work and produce for the colony was welcome. As Jews in Amsterdam were major funders of the Dutch West India and Dutch East India companies, it is known that this fact had some impact on the reply. (New Netherlands, as mentioned in the letter, was the large Dutch colony that extended from the Delaware River to Albany, New York, to southern Connecticut, and included New Amsterdam.)

Despite the more open position of the Dutch West India Company, there was still much disquiet by parts of the population (particularly the more religious component) regarding Jews. A Reverend Johannes Megapolensis wrote in March 18, 1655 to his superiors in Amsterdam that the Jews currently in New Amsterdam: "...Report that many more of the same lot would follow, and then they would build a synagogue. This causes among the congregation here a great deal of complaint and murmuring. These people have no other God than the Mammon of unrighteousness, and no other aim than to get possession of Christian property, and to overcome all other merchants by drawing all trade towards themselves..." And he added that he was greatly troubled if the "...obstinate and immovable Jews..." and "godless rascals" came to settle here.[9]

A Hebrew congregation was rapidly organized in New Amsterdam – probably no later than 1655. The first Torah was brought to the colony from Amsterdam by Abraham de Lucena. A cemetery for Jews was approved in 1656 in a "little hook of land outside of the city," but the location of this initial cemetery is not known.[10] Despite allowing the Jews to stay, the local council tried to thwart the newcomer's activities in trading with Indians on the Delaware River and the Hudson River. In 1655 Jews requested permission to trade at Ft. Orange, (Albany), but were denied by the governor, with a note that if any trading had taken place the Jews "needed to dispose of their goods and then return thither." The restrictions on engaging in shopkeeping and trades were carryovers of the widespread Guild system in Europe, which essentially formed a "closed shop," limiting and controlling outside participation. The Jews appealed to the Dutch West India Company in Amsterdam, and replies in March and June 1656 stated that Jews had the right to trade, and even to possess real estate (a major step forward), except "they are not to be employed in any public service or retail business," and they could not conduct public worship services. In fact no religion other than the Dutch Reformed Church could practice their religion openly in New Amsterdam. The restriction on retail business (which was not in the earlier company reply) was troublesome as it was thought that its basis was to protect the Christian business community from competition. Essentially, the Jews disregarded the restriction where possible, and in fact did expand areas of activity to the Hudson and Delaware Rivers and other areas in the northeast.

As a result of this reply from Amsterdam, Asser Levy, (a butcher by trade), and one of the most visible and dynamic newcomers, proceeded to buy property in Albany. Stuyvesant was always concerned about an adequate defense for the colony. In 1653 he built a wall along what would later be Wall Street to protect against incursions by the Indians and British, and established a plan for guard duty by the citizens. But the governor had imposed a tax on Jews in lieu of their standing guard duty over the colony. He wrote that "...the nation (Jews) shall remain exempt from the several training and guard duties, on condition that each male person contribute for the aforesaid freedom toward the relief of the general municipal taxes 65 stivers..."

Jews guarding his colony was clearly not Stuyvesant's style. He felt that they had the benefit of the colony's fortification, and had sufficient civic rights. Levy and Barsimon aggressively pressed their right to participate as other citizens do in keeping "watch and ward," rather than simply accepting Stuyvesant's "freedom" by paying the specialized tax. They wanted to serve but were rejected. They chose a confrontation with Stuyvesant to gain their civic rights and duties.

The records of New Amsterdam for November 8, 1655 state that: "Jacob Barsimon and Asser Levy request to be permitted to keep guard with other burghers, or be free from the tax which others of their nation pay, as they must earn their living as manual laborers."

The vote of Stuyvesant and the council were noted as: "Director General and Council persist in the resolution, yet as the petitioners are of the opinion that the results will be injurious to them, consent is hereby given to them to depart whenever and whither it pleases them."[11]

They chose not to take the sly suggestion to leave the colony, but appealed the decision. They were later accepted as guards.

But Asser Levy did not rest. In April 1657 Levy was again pressing the colony to accept him (and others) as full and equal citizens. The record reads: "Asser Levy, a Jew, appears in Court; requests to be admitted a Burgher; claims that such ought not to be refused him as he keeps watch and ward like other Burghers; showing a Burgher certificate from the City of Amsterdam that the Jew is Burgher there. Which being deliberated on, it is decreed, as before, that it cannot be allowed, and he shall apply to the Director General and Council."

He appealed (as you would expect) to the governmental council and Stuyvesant, and, amazingly, only ten days later Jews were admitted as citizens. These extraordinarily important positions that Asser Levy and Jacob Barsimon continually took to defend their rights in the 1650s were the first of many legal battles that Jews in America would undertake in asserting their civil and political rights.

In October 1655 Stuyvesant in a letter to the Board of the Dutch West India Company in Amsterdam stated that: "To give liberty to the Jews will be very detrimental there, because the Christians there will not be able at the same time to do business. Giving them liberty, we cannot refuse the Lutherans and the Papists."[12] Besides this concern, things were really starting to look bleak for Stuyvesant in more ways than one.

One possible explanation for the turnaround in policy that would allow Levy and Barsimon to serve and receive citizenship was that the British had started looking covetously at New Amsterdam. People were coming in greater numbers to New England, Virginia and Maryland, the areas surrounding New Netherlands. The colony needed every able-bodied person (even Jews) for its defense and support. By the 1660s both the Jewish community and the colony in general, were in serious decline. With the colony's decline the atmosphere of New Amsterdam's government towards Jews and Christian dissidents was becoming slightly less hostile. The colony did not make money for the Dutch West India Company, which viewed the colony as a poor investment, and never adequately defended it. The colony was in a survival mode.

Efforts had been made over the years to strengthen the colony by trying to increase immigration as well as increasing agricultural activity. In the last years of the colony there were even programs to bring boys and girls (generally ages 12-20) from Dutch poorhouses and orphan asylums. Stuyvesant was not a supporter of this effort; he felt that most children "are more inclined to carry a beggar's gripsack than to labor." The birthrate and the flow of new immigrants never kept up with the more rapid growth of the English population in New England, Virginia and Maryland. The Jews remained essentially no more than a handful of people within the population, and Jews began to leave for Amsterdam and the Caribbean.

The British took over New Netherlands in 1664 without a fight. The English Colonel Richard Nicholls (who became New York's first governor) had four warships sitting in the harbor ready to invade. He gave the Dutch two days to surrender, and they did. The Torah scroll, received in 1655, was returned to Amsterdam. Stuyvesant was recalled to Amsterdam to explain why he surrendered without firing a shot. He then returned to New Amsterdam (now New York), and retired to his fruit farm in Manhattan. He died in 1672, and is buried as Petrus Stuyvesant in lower Manhattan. (Stuyvesant's wall on Wall Street would come down in 1699.)

The burial site was on his farm, now where St. Marks-in-the-Bowery is located, near 2nd Avenue and 10th Street. His grave is very near the well-known 2*nd Avenue Deli,* and only a few blocks from the district where the Yiddish theater blossomed for years. Stuyvesant was never able to stay as far away from Jews as he really wanted.

But a squabble over the territory lingered despite the Dutch surrender. A series of Anglo-Dutch wars ensued, mainly stemming from commercial rivalry over lucrative overseas commerce. There was no goodwill between the two. Finally, the Treaty of Breda in 1667 ended the dispute over New Amsterdam with the British permanently retaining New Amsterdam (including New Jersey and Delaware), and the Dutch getting Surinam in South America. At the time of the takeover by the British there were almost no Jews left in New Amsterdam. Some said Asser Levy was the last one remaining after the British took over in 1664. Most Jews had departed over the years due to Stuyvesant's general hostility. They came only in small numbers, apparently choosing to go to other more hospitable areas, such as the West Indies. (Most Jews in colonial times were highly mobile, as events, opportunities, obstacles or potential dangers appeared.)

A copper marker near a flagpole at the intersection of State and Whitehall Streets in New York City commemorates the historic initial landing of the Jews in 1654. It reads: "Erected by the State of New York to honor the memory of the twenty-three men, women and children who landed in September 1654 and founded the first Jewish community in North America."

6B

BRITISH NEW YORK, AMERICAN NEW YORK, AND SHEARITH ISRAEL

The British changed the name to New York. But it certainly was not "Hatapuach Hagadol" (The Big Apple) as yet for the Jews. Peter Stuyvesant was not in charge, but things were slow to change for the very few Jews who might have remained in the British colony. The city's population was now about 1,500. As the number of Jews slowly increased, they were not permitted to open retail businesses (a rule disregarded in many cases); own real estate; hold public office; or worship in public. But they did continue trade with the Indians (as was done previously), not necessarily with legal approval.

A few years after the British took over, promotional material that served as guide books appeared describing "New York formerly called New Amsterdam," noting "the fertility of the land, Healthfulness of the Climate and the Commodities thense produced." The guide gave "Advise to those as come thither; An account of what commodities they should take with them," as well as "A Brief Relation of the Customs of the Indians there."

By taking over New Netherlands King Charles II and his brother, James, the Duke of York, hoped to enlarge their American domain, as well as weaken the economically aggressive and flourishing Dutch empire. To demonstrate the concern the British had regarding the Dutch, the British renamed what is now the *Hudson River,* the *North River*. Henry Hudson, an Englishman, was the first European to travel the river, but his discovery was made while he was an employee of the Dutch. The British were concerned that using the term *Hudson River* could lend some possible support to any future Dutch territorial claims, and they preferred not to use the term for quite a period of time. It was many years before Dutch maps regularly acknowledged the transfer of the territory.

The diversity in population remained. Alan Taylor quotes an English New Yorker complaining in 1692 that, "Our chiefest unhappynes (sic) here is too great a mixture of nations, and English the least part." The restriction on Jews in retail trade continued. However, the colonies needed to foster commerce, and with the complexity of enforcing any controls, many business projects went on despite legal restrictions. The Charter of Liberty and Privileges of 1683 again limited some benefits to colonists not professing Christianity, a continuing theme in early New York. But Jews were clearly pushing the system to gain whatever opportunities and rights they could.

A statement by the Duke of York in 1674 was rather amazing for the time. He told the governor of New York to "permit all persons of what religion so ever, quietly to inhabitt within the precincts of yo'r jurisdiccion w'thout giving them any disturbance or disquiet whatsoever for or by reason of their differing opinion in matter of Religion."[13]

A cemetery was purchased by the community in 1682, located near Chatham Square (just south of Chinatown), only about 250 ft. from the intersection of Oliver Street and St. James Place. Graves were relocated to other cemeteries in 1791-2, due to earth sliding, and in 1855-6, due to road construction. Thus, only a portion of the 1682 cemetery remains. A new cemetery was purchased in 1729 on Gold Street. The original 1656 cemetery "on a little hook of land" has never been located.

In 1682 Domine Selyns wrote that Quakers and Jews and others held "...separate meetings," indicating that religious services were taking place. Services probably took place earlier than 1682 in British New York, but proof is uncertain. In 1685 the Jews petitioned for the right to conduct their services openly, but were once again told by the British governor that public worship was only for those who profess a faith in Christ. Nevertheless, an observer in 1692 disclosed that Jews "had their own church" on the south side of Beaver Street, between Broadway and Broad Street. A Miller Plan map, printed in 1696, clearly designates this house synagogue. (The original map is currently at the British Library, London.) Between 1695 and 1699 there were 100-150 Jews in New York in a city of about 5000; Jews paying taxes increased from eight or nine to fourteen.

Although commercial and religious restrictions were not rescinded in New York, the Jews nevertheless integrated into the commercial sectors and into retail, artisan and craft occupations. There is clear evidence that by 1700 the house synagogue had moved to Mill Street. By 1706 Congregation Shearith Israel was formally established with a constitution. Services were held in a rented building at a cost of £8 a year. Mill Street by that time was commonly called "Jews Alley."

Jacob Marcus believes that some interim congregations had very short existences, which apparently did occur in colonial times. He notes a short-lived congregation in New York, no later than 1720, called Shearith Yaacob (Remnant of Jacob). An important step forward in religious equality took place after the death of George I. By 1727 Jews were able to take the oath of allegiance to the crown without the words "upon the faith of a Christian." By 1729 Shearith Israel was ready to build a synagogue. They set about soliciting funds (a truly eternal enterprise) from existing Jewish communities in the Caribbean and London. A letter, in Spanish, dated January 16, 1729 was sent from Shearith Israel to the Jewish congregation in Jamaica, stating in part:

> "We earnestly request you all as well as your haham (rabbi) to communicate it to members of your holy Kaal (congregation), so that they may contribute all they can to the building of a holy synagogue which we have decided with the help of God to erect. We have alredy (sic) purchased an appropriate site for the edifice and (for another) cemetery, but for want of sufficient means, the Yehudim (Jews) here being but few, we have not been able to carry out our intention, and until our hopes are realized, we must continue for the present to congregate in a synagogue rented from a goy (Gentile). May the Almighty grant our wish, and may He move your hearts that you may to the best of your ability assist us in the matter, and also help us build a fence around the cemetery. . ."[14]

Both Sephardim and Askenazim cooperated in building the synagogue; both groups believing it was time to move from rented spaces. There were an estimated 75 Jewish families in New York, about 37 active members – 15 Sephardim and 22 Ashkenazim. Even though the Ashkenazim were the majority, the Sephardic *minhag* (Spanish and Portuguese form of worship) was adopted, a standard that was followed in the colonial synagogues.

The first synagogue in what would become the United States was built in 1729-30 on Mill Street in New York. Financial assistance came from synagogues in Jamaica, Barbados, Bevis Marks in London, Curaçao and Dutch Guinea. Mikvé Israel in Curaçao tried to obtain assurances, in a long and legal sounding letter, that the Sephardim would maintain control of the synagogue. The Curaçao Jews actually requested a signed agreement from the Sephardic and Ashkenazim attesting to this requirement. It is not known whether a confirming reply was ever sent.

Although this first synagogue, consecrated on April 8, 1730, was a small building, it was actually larger than the Baptist and Quaker meeting houses. It measured 35′ x 35′ and 21′ high. A balcony for women ran around three sides. There was also a mikvah (ritual bath), the water coming from a spring that also powered mills on the appropriately named Mill Street.[15] The property had been purchased for £100 and one loaf of sugar and one pound of tea.

The face of the building was blue-faced brick, with a peaked and sloping roof on all four sides. There was a tall central door on the north side, light came in from windows on all sides, except the eastern wall. There were five chandeliers: four sixteen-candle chandeliers in each corner and a thirty-two candle chandelier in the center. Synagogue minutes were taken for a short period in Portuguese, then both Portuguese and English, and, finally, just English.

It is interesting to note that Sephardic congregations generally tried to run a very tightly controlled synagogue, with an apparently long list of rules and associated fines. While they varied from synagogue to synagogue, there were specific fines for chatting during services; for putting away the tallis (prayer shawl) before the conclusion of the service; for singing louder than the hazzan; for leaving the synagogue without permission of the president or an officer; for not attending a service or being late, and for not accepting an honor offered by the synagogue.

In a more humorous note a fine was imposed in a Baltimore congregation for chewing tobacco. But to be on the safe side, the congregation installed spittoons. The failure of the membership to adhere to congregational rules may have been a significant source of funding!

A day school was formed by Shearith Israel in 1731; the teacher's salary was a load of wood per year plus 8 shillings per quarter for each student. By 1747 school was in session 9am – 12 noon daily, and 2pm – 5pm on Thursdays.[16] This is the first Hebrew School in the colonies, and after a time the study of Spanish and arithmetic was added. Where synagogues existed, Jews, if they desired, received some generally meager Hebrew education. In some later colonies, Hebrew, if taught at all, was done by tutors rather than in formal schools, and the cost of private tutors probably precluded a Hebrew education for many.

When there was a need for a hazzan in 1757, letters were sent to Congregation Sharei Hashamayim (Bevis Marks) in London. Originally the request was for an unmarried hazzan (to cut down transportation and salary costs) who knew Hebrew, English and Spanish. A return letter stated that such a person could not be found at this time. Shearith Israel responded on March 13, 1758 modifying its request:

> "...wee have no Objection to a marr'ed man, but would choose one rather if with a Small Family, and not Attended with much Charge, as our congregation is Small, and few that are Able to Contribute to the Support Thereof. . .The salary of Fifty Pounds Sterling is Exclusive of Voluntary offerings, Marriages and other things of that kind... Should a proper person present wee Shall defray the reasonable Expense of thire (sic) sea store (food on the voyage) and Passage. . .As to settling a salary for a term of years or returning at our expense, on any little (disagreement) which he Might take, it is not agreeable to the congregation, and wee Presume might be attended with bad consequences. . .But we think there will be no reason to doubt his Continuance Should he not Misbehave, which wee hope will Not happen, as wee are Confident that your goodness would not Recomend any but Such as may Appear proper and worthy."[17]

Another letter that same day to Moses Franks in London, who was assisting in the process of obtaining a hazzan, stated:

> "...Should they Nominate any Person Worthy of Thire Recommendation to Come over in the Carictor of a Hazzan for our congregation. Desire youl be pleasd, to Supply him with as much as may be reasonable to lay in a deceant Sea Stire and Pay...wee Conclude wishing you a Merry Holyday, with health and posperity..."

The 1730 Mill St. synagogue was replaced in 1758 with a building on the same street. A year later Joseph Jessuran Pinto was recommended by the London synagogue, and was hired as hazzan, as well as a teacher of Hebrew to the general community. The following year there was a move to hire a teacher specifically for the children, and they turned to the Jewish community in the Caribbean. Apparently there seems to have been a paucity of local talent. A December 1760 letter to Benjamin Pereira in Jamaica requested his assistance in hiring if possible:

> "...a Suitable Master Capable to Teach our Children ye Hebrew language. English & Spanish he ought to know: but he will not Suit us unless he understands Hebrew and English at Least: this must Require your particular care: A Single, modest: Sober: person will be most agreeable however on your good Judgeemnt wee shall depend as you Very well know our minds and Tempers. . .Children whose parents are in needy Circumstances he must Teach Gratis. His salary shall be first at fourty pounds, New York money p(er) year........and all other children he teaches must and will pay him as has been done heretofore. Wee flatter ourselves you will Excuse the Trouble wee give you. . ."

Gershom Mendes Seixas was elected chazan/reader/"rabbi" of Shearith Israel in 1768, when he was just twenty-two. His father came from Lisbon to New York some thirty years earlier and was a merchant. His mother was born in New York.

Seixas' election was due to both his competence and the apparent lack of other "qualified" applicants. He was born in New York in 1745 of a Sephardi father and Ashkanzi mother. His maternal grandfather, Moses Levy, lived in London, an owner of merchant vessels who migrated to New York in 1701 and became involved with Shearith Israel. Levy's daughter, born in the United States, married Isaac Mendes Seixas; Gershom was one of their six children. Seixas kept up the tradition of large families, and twelve children would result from his two marriages.

He, like all religious leaders of the colonial synagogues, were not trained rabbis. The degree of education – formal or informal – varied. They were called hazzan (one who chants or reads the prayers), or Reverend, or chacham (learned one). These religious functionaries were generally kept on a very tight rein by the local board of trustees or the president. They generally were hired to lead the services and to teach Hebrew school, and in many cases were expected to perform a number of additional jobs, including being shochet (ritual slaughterer) and mohel (performer of circumcisions). While many were inadequately trained, they were generally the most competent religious authority on the scene, and considering that many of the congregants had little or no formal religious training in the Torah and Talmud, they really could hardly judge their religious figures competence in areas of Jewish doctrine. In some communities they were not treated with full respect.

Seixas was an exception to the normal synagogue hazzan of those times. He had both the intellectual depth to address some religious issues and rabbinic lore, but he was not well trained in Hebrew. His records indicate that his Hebrew knowledge was limited on his becoming hazzan; his Hebrew writing contained many grammatical errors. He was an excellent speaker, and able to bring messages of Judaism to a wide audience and interact most effectively with the Jewish and non-Jewish communities.

Seixas remained the spiritual leader of Shearith Israel from 1768 to 1776, and from 1784 to 1816, with a most distinguished and fruitful tenure. The break in time was due to his residence in Stamford, Connecticut and then Philadelphia, during the Revolutionary War, where he was involved in building Mikveh Israel.

Seixas supplemented his income by tutoring Hebrew, and by performing circumcisions. (Not until 1840 did an ordained rabbi take a pulpit in the United States, at the Baltimore Hebrew Congregation).

Seixas served the American revolutionary cause with strong passion; his speeches overflowed with ideas and energy. Most of the preachers in New York were Tories, supporting the British as the Revolutionary War approached. But not Seixas.

In August 1776, concerned about the dangers to New York with the British on Long Island, Seixas preached a patriotic sermon, and closed the synagogue, taking the Torahs and silver and candlesticks to his father-in-law's home in Stamford, Connecticut. While most of the synagogue's members were patriots, a few of the congregants were Tories – who were considered "rabble" by the "rebels" opposing the British.

Most Jews fled New York during the British occupation, some to Connecticut, but many going south to Philadelphia where they called for their hazzan to join them – which he did. Seixas spent the Revolutionary War period in Philadelphia. As a result, Isaac Touro, who was loyal to the British, journeyed from Rhode Island to New York to try to lead Shearith Israel during the period of British occupation, and when that did not occur, he sailed for Kingston, Jamaica.

Seixas was one of the clergymen who participated in George Washington's presidential inauguration in New York in November 1789, and in that same year, he attended a large affair when Pennsylvania approved the United

States Constitution

In 1784 the members of Shearith Israel requested Seixas' return to New York. Mikveh Israel in Philadelphia requested a delay of several months, but Shearith Israel forcefully pressed for his return, which he did within a matter of two weeks, despite Seixas himself requesting a delay, stating he was ill.

He was reelected hazzan at an annual salary of £200, 6 cords of hickory wood and £6 and 8 shillings for the trip back from Philadelphia. Following the period spent in Philadelphia, Seixas immediately started some changes in his synagogue, one of which was to substitute the use of English for Portuguese or Spanish, wherever it supplemented Hebrew. In his sermons (and some say in the service) he used English instead of Portuguese. But he always remained Orthodox, and most probably did not conceive of the future Reform movement. It is very hard to believe that he would have, or could have, approved of it at all. Seixas invited Episcopal clergy to sit near him at Shearith Israel, and was one of the original incorporators of Columbia College, (now Columbia University). He was a trustee for 30 years, and the college struck a medal in his honor at its 175th anniversary. In August 1800 he even preached a sermon at St. Paul's Episcopal Church, a most unusual occurrence. He was also elected to the first Board of Regents by the New York State legislature.

A translation from Hebrew into English of the New Year and Yom Kippur services appeared in 1761 by an anonymous author, who actually was Isaac Pinto of New York. Five years later he published under his own name a *Sabbath, Rosh Hashanah and Yom Kippur* service translation. He noted the necessity for an English prayer book inasmuch as Hebrew "is imperfectly understood by many, and by some not at all," and he hoped the translation would "tend to the improvement of many of my Bretheren in their Devotion."

His work preceeded by some sixty or more years the similar concepts of The Reformed Society of Israelites in Charleston, and Isaac Harby, Abraham Moïse and Isaac M. Wise. But apparently he also preceeded any demand for such volumes; neither found much of an audience, nor were they used in any services at the time. There did not seem to be any opposition to such translations, but, then again, there were few readers.

Pinto was an excellent linguist. In 1786 he was hired as a Spanish interpreter by the Federal Department of Foreign Affairs and the U.S. Congress. After three years he felt he was being inadequately compensated and wrote to the Secretary of State John Jay in 1789, who responded that he was shortly leaving office and advised Pinto to write his successor, Thomas Jefferson. He did, but we have seen no record of the outcome.

Seixas also created some transliterations, so worshipers could keep track of their place during services. The availability of transliterations as well as the availability of translations (which apparently were not used) put the Orthodox of that time on guard; their concern was that some people may eventually be seeking changes in the services. A draft of a 1790 Shearith Israel regulation stated: "that no language (was) to be made use of in synagogue but Hebrew, except for the offering."[18]

It may be of interest to note, that despite the many strengths Gershom Seixas brought to Shearith Israel, he apparently could not motivate the desire of parents to support Hebrew education for their children. When their new school was opened in 1804, none of the parents responded, and the Board of Trustees announced, "few, very few indeed, are concerned about it."

The Sephardim/Ashkenazi differences were in most instances contained and rarely interfered or harmed the community. The antagonisms between the two groups in the early United States generally exacerbated in the 1800s, when there were larger number of Jews in the country and a more rapidly expanding Ashkenazi population. In times of communal need religious differences seemed to be pushed aside. But as times became more comfortable, the old differences became more contentious.

By the 1820s Shearith Israel was concerned that with the increase of Ashkenazim in New York there was a possibility that new members may gain control and change the form of prayer service. Believing that the congregation was about to apply rules that would control the admittance of new members, a group who desired the Ashkenazi services formed Congregation B'nai Jeshurun in 1825. This was the first Ashkenazi synagogue in New York, and only the second synagogue in the city. The new congregation stated its belief that "...a large portion of our bretheren who have been educated in the German and Polish minhag, who find it difficult to accustom themselves to what is familiarly known as the Portuguese minhag, in consequence of their earlier impressions and habits."

In 1834 Shearith Israel moved again, this time to Crosby Street into a building boasting the wonders of gas lighting. The move was primarily due to the northward migration of the city's residential community. In retrospect, it was quite fortuitous. A fire on Mill Street two years later would have consumed the synagogue; the street was completely destroyed.

The Congregation Shearith Israel is also known as the Spanish and Portuguese Synagogue. After a series of moves, it finally settled at its current location on Central Park West and West 70th Street. Gershom Mendes Seixas died in 1816, and is buried in the Chatham Square cemetery on St. James Place. Eighteen Revolutionary War soldiers are also buried there.

6C

THE TOURO SYNAGOGUE IN NEWPORT, RHODE ISLAND

Meanwhile, another pioneering congregation and synagogue was coming into place in Newport, Rhode Island, a very important seaport at that time. Newport was a thriving community under the tolerant founder, Roger Williams. He believed in religious liberty. Williams was banished in 1635 from Puritan Massachusetts, and one year later established in Providence, Rhode Island a government devoid of civil power over religious matters, with religious liberty for the inhabitants. He believed that civil authority did not have power over one's conscience. It was a refuge from religious persecution that was rampant at that time — particularly in the Massachusetts Bay Colony.

Newport was founded in 1639, and by 1646 it was an important port for shipbuilding and foreign commerce. Williams went to England in 1643 trying to gain the right to consolidate Portsmouth, Newport, Warwick and Providence into a colony. It was granted, then rescinded in 1651, but then restored once more.

A Code of Laws in 1647 stated in part:

"These are the laws that concerne all men. . .and otherwise what is herein forbidden, all men may walk as their conciences (sic) persuade them, everyone in the name of his God."[19]

To most that may sound good, but conservative Protestants called his Rhode Island "the receptacle of riff-raff people. . .Nothing else than the sewer of New England."

Jews and Quakers came there, starting in the late 1650s. It is believed that some 15 families, including Mordecai Campenell and Moses Pacheco, came from Curaçao in 1658; others came from Amsterdam (and possibly New York) in 1658. A royal charter stating there would be absolute liberty of conscience was granted in 1663. By 1677, some 20 years after their arrival, there was "sold . . . unto Mordicay Campanall and Moses Pacheckoe, Jews and to their nation, society and friends, a peice (sic) of land for a burial place."[20] The Newport cemetery was enlarged in 1768 and still exists in its entirety.

By about the 1680s the Jewish community, many of Barbadian extraction, drifted away; some went to New York and others to Barbados. The possible reasons are many, one being that they felt that there would be no economic future in the colony due to highly restrictive British trading and shipping laws. But some stayed on, and there were additional colonists by the 1690s.

Ninety Jews came from Curaçao in 1694, escaping from an epidemic. Additional people came from other islands in the West Indies, but only about one-third remained. It is known there was a Jews Street in Newport in 1702. By 1705 Jews introduced soap making into Rhode Island. Jacob Rivera founded the sperm whale oil industry and with others introduced spermaceti – then invaluable for candles. Restrictive laws against Jews and Catholics were in place by 1715, and many Jews left. In time, trade increased, particularly with New York, when Jews came from New York in the 1740s and 1750s. There were also arrivals from Jamaica in 1750.

By the 1760s there were seventeen candle factories in Newport with trade and manufacturing agreements between them and factories in New England and Philadelphia, that seemed to establish a cartel arrangement, with plans to control costs, prices, and an integrated form of product distribution. They agreed not to manufacture for others, and were by "all fair and honorable means" to prevent the growth of competition. They called themselves the United Company of Spermaceti Candlers. But there were enough price undercuttings by cartel members to cause the cartel to fail.

By 1759 a cornerstone was laid for a synagogue. The architect, of what is now considered a masterpiece, was Peter Harrison, who was born in England, came to Newport in 1740 and became a most notable architect in mid-18th century America. His design philosophy seems closely tied to Christopher Wren, the English architect, and Andrea Palladio of Italy. Harrison designed the synagogue in Palladian style, its beauty enhanced by its classical symmetry and balance with some internal modifications to accommodate Sephardic religious requirements. Five massive candelabra hang from the ceiling dated 1765; two others are dated 1760 and 1770.

Money was not easy to raise. A letter noted great disappointment "in the expectations from the charity of other congregations" with the cost rising "too much. . .more than it was conceived." This could have been written today. Bevis Marks' reply contained no donations, but they did send two donation boxes and a letter ending, "May God be the one who assists all. . .and may He prosper you in your pious plans. " There followed a fairly long period of gathering funds some of which came from Shearith Israel in New York and some from Curaçao and Surinam. A Torah was borrowed from Shearith Israel.

Isaac Touro came to Newport in 1760 from Amsterdam, having been recommended by that city's Portuguese synagogue, and became Newport synagogue's first leader. (He also spent some time in Jamaica.) His religious education was in Amsterdam. Like the religious leaders in America at that time, he was not a rabbi. Ground was broken for the synagogue in 1759, six cornerstones were laid, but the building was not completed and dedicated until December 2, 1763. It was formally named Yeshuat Yisroel (Salvation of Israel), but commonly known today as the Touro Synagogue, named after its first (and only leader) during its initial period of use. A deerskin Torah was given to the congregation by the Portuguese synagogue in Amsterdam.

Newport Jews used the name Kahal Kodesh Nefutse (or Nephutsay)Yisroel (The Scattered of Israel) prior to adopting Yeshuat Yisroel. With the synagogue in place they possibly no longer felt scattered.

While the synagogue is a most beautiful one, its first congregation used it for only about 13 years, before leaving the city during the Revolutionary War. Isaac Touro left early in the war (as did almost all Jews in Newport in 1776). The British captured the city and retained the city from 1776-1779. They confiscated merchant ships and destroyed many buildings.

It is estimated that about one-third of all colonists were loyalists supporting the British, about one-third were patriots supporting the attempt to replace the British and one-third seemed rather ambivalent to the whole historic event. In 1776 the Rhode Island Assembly tried to get loyalty oaths to determine who had British Loyalist leanings. Some refused to answer on the grounds that not everyone was subjected to this "test." Isaac Touro (listed as a "Jew Priest") refused, saying he was never naturalized, thus still Dutch, and, secondly, he believed that a loyalty oath was against his religious principles. But, in fact, Touro was a supporter of the British, unsympathetic to American independence.[21] And he was far from alone. For example, Benjamin Franklin's illegitimate son, William, was the Royal Governor of New Jersey and strongly opposed the patriots.[22] He headed the "Associated Loyalists" in New York and Perth Amboy. William was jailed in Connecticut and eventually sent to England.

Touro went from Newport to New York, another British held area. Aware that the patriotic Gershon Mendes Seixas had left New York for Stamford, Connecticut and then later Philadelphia, Touro tried to lead Shearith Israel in New York. Unable to find a pulpit in New York, he fled to another British territory, Kingston, Jamaica, where he died in 1783 at the age of 46.

His widow and their children then travelled to Boston, where they stayed with one of her brothers. The children, Judah and Abraham, would prove to be most successful businessmen, but also most prodigious philanthropists to Jewish and other causes.

When President George Washington visited Newport in August 17, 1790, the warden of the Touro Synagogue, Moses Seixas (one of the founders of the Bank of Rhode Island), wrote a letter to the president, which said, in part:

> "Deprived as we have heretofore been of the invaluable rights of free Citizens, we now, (with a deep sense of gratitude to the Almighty dispenser of all events) behold a Government erected by the Majesty of the People – a Government, which to bigotry gives no sanction, to persecution no assistance – but generously affording to All liberty of conscience, and immunities of Citizenship. . ."[23]
>
> Moses Seixas, *Warden*

A few days later, August 21st, Washington's reply was received, which, strikingly, contained almost the exact words written by Moses Seixas:

> ". . .the Government of the United States, which gives to bigotry no sanction, to persecution no assistance requires only that they who live under its protection should demean themselves as good citizens. . .May the Children of the Stock of Abraham, who dwell in this land continue to merit and enjoy the good will of the other Inhabitants; while everone shall sit in the safety under his own vine and figtree, and there shall be none to make him afraid. . ."
>
> G. Washington

Washington's stirring and historic words, essentially quoted from Seixas' letter, occurred at a time when Newport's Jewish community was in serious decline. Jews had returned after the war in small numbers; services were restarted but ended in 1792. The city was rapidly losing its Jewish population to Providence, New York, Philadelphia, Virginia and South Carolina. Newport itself was becoming a backwater to Providence and would never regain its economic importance. The synagogue building became a city government facility as well as the state's General Assembly. It gradually went into disrepair. By 1820, barely a handful of Jews remained in Newport.

Shearith Israel wrote to Newport in 1818 that "for a great number of years past there has not been a service in the synagogue in the Newport and the Seapharim (sic) (Torah Scrolls)...(are) in the house of the late Mr. Moses Seixas for more than twenty years." It requested their return, but noted that the Scrolls would be available when services resumed. Shearith Israel was given title to the closed synagogue, cemetery and other property and that title is still in effect. The four Torah Scrolls were sent to New York in 1833.[24]

In 1840 Rabbi Abraham Rice, newly arrived from Europe, who studied in Germany, came to Baltimore and then traveled to Newport to revitalize the synagogue. Isaac Fine notes that Rice found a negligible Jewish population, so he returned to Baltimore to become the rabbi at the Baltimore Hebrew Congregation – the first ordained rabbi to have a pulpit in the United States. A writer of the times observed that the Touro Synagogue "was left to the bats and moles and to the occasional invasion...of boys who took pleasure in examining the furniture scattered about." Services started again, intermittently, in the 1850s, generally during the summers. By 1883 Touro was reopened on a year-round basis and rededicated. But periods of inactivity, nevertheless, ensued.

The sons of Isaac Touro, Abraham and Judah, did play vital roles in the preservation of the Touro synagogue and cemetery. Theodore Lewis notes that Abraham Touro was funding the preservation of the empty synagogue by 1820, when there were almost no Jews in Newport. Abraham was a merchant and shipbuilder in Boston who would leave large bequests to preserve the building. He also built many roads in the Boston area, and supported a number of hospitals, including Massachussetts General. He died at the age of 48 in a carriage accident.

The other son, Judah, even surpassed his brother in extraordinary generosity. Judah, one of the first Jews in New Orleans, acquired a significant fortune as a shipbuilder and merchant as well, and gave generously to both Jewish and non-Jewish causes. He donated $10,000 towards the Bunker Hill Monument. The organization raising funds for the monument had almost given up the project due to the lack of adequate donations. Touro gave the money desiring that it be an unknown gift, matching an equal gift by Amos Laurance of Boston. Upon receiving the check from an unknown person in New Orleans, the monument committee initially considered it a hoax. At the monument's dedication a poem was read, which ended:

Christian and Jew, they carry out a plan,
For though of different faith, each is in heart a man.

Judah's generosity, both in life and in his will, made him the first broad-based philanthropist in this country. He even purchased a church that was in financial difficulty and allowed the congregation to remain rent free. He died in 1854 at the age of 79. His will contained over 60 bequests, and $500,000 in donations (equivalent to $10 million today) to synagogues as far away as St. Louis, Cincinnati and Albany, New York and to orphanages, asylums and churches of various faiths. He gave $5,000 each to Shearith Israel in Charleston and Mickve Israel in Savannah, and $50,000 to Moses Montifiore "to ameliorate the conditions of our unfortunate Jewish Bretheren in the Holy Land." Another $10,000 was given for salaries for those conducting services at the Newport synagogue as well as for care of the cemetery.

Isaac Leeser at the end of his eulogy to Judah Touro said "...He, the merchant in the far West (New Orleans), who had lived for years separated from his people, almost a solitary worshipper of one God, forgot not those who still linger on the soil consecrated by so many wonderful events which marked our early history, to cheer them on in their deprivations, to which they are subjected." His tombstone in the Newport cemetery reads in part: *By righteousness and integrity he collected his wealth in charity and for salvation he dispensed it.*

Henry Wadsworth Longfellow wrote a poem, *The Jewish Cemetery in Newport.* Four of the stanzas are quoted below, which pay tribute to the Sephardi and Ashkenazi Jews who were part of the initial immigration to America:

How strange it seems. These Hebrews in their graves,
Close by the street of this fair seaport town,
Silent besides the never-silent waves,
At rest in all this moving up and down.

The very names recorded here are strange,
Of foreign accent, and of different climes;
Alvares and Rivera interchange
With Abraham and Jacob of old times.

How came they here? What burst of Christian hate,
What persecution, merciless and blind,
Drove o'er the sea – that desert desolate –
These Ishmaels and Hagars of mankind.

They lived in narrow streets and lanes obscure,
Ghetto and Judenstrass, in mirk and mire;

Taught in the school of patience to endure
The life of anguish and the death of fire.

It is now an Orthodox synagogue, as well as a famous tourist site and a National Landmark. The Touro Synagogue is the oldest synagogue building still standing in the United States. Kahal Kadosh Beth Elohim in Charleston, South Carolina follows in second place with its present 1841 synagogue.

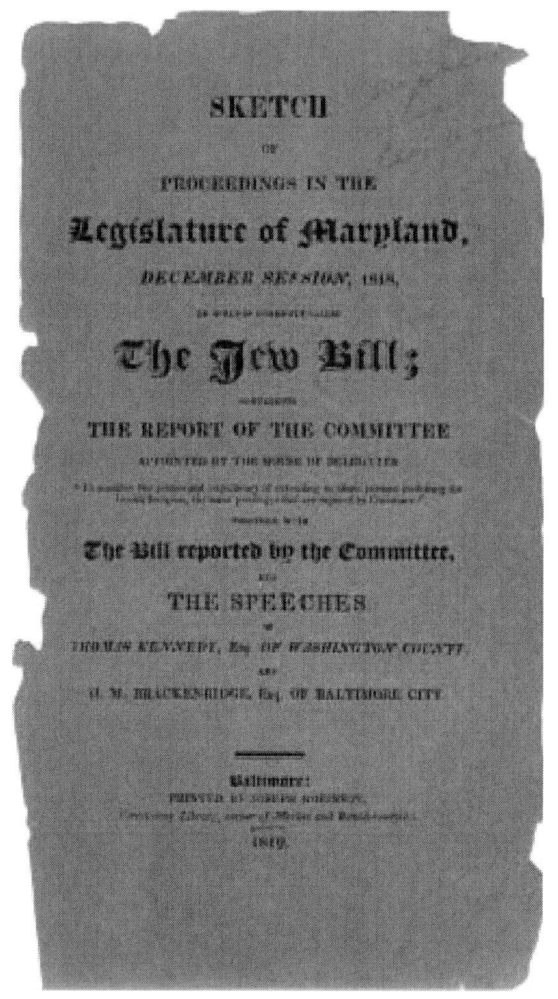

SKETCH

OF

PROCEEDINGS IN THE

Legislature of Maryland,

DECEMBER SESSION, 1818,

The Jew Bill;

THE REPORT OF THE COMMITTEE

The Bill reported by the Committee,

AND

THE SPEECHES

OF

THOMAS KENNEDY, Esq. OF WASHINGTON COUNTY,

AND

H. M. BRACKENRIDGE, Esq. OF BALTIMORE CITY

Baltimore:

1819.

Cover of Maryland's 1818 Jew Bill legislation.
Courtesy of Jewish Museum of Maryland, Baltimore, MD

View of city of New Amsterdam, circa 1655.
Courtesy of the New York Public Library; Astor, Lenox and Tilden Foundations

1730 Carwitham Plan of New York City. Printed in 1740. 1682 Jewish cemetery is located at the western edge of "Swamp Meadow." A drawing of Shearith Israel's 1730 Mill St. synagogue is circled on the map.

Courtesy of Lord Leicester and Trustees of the Holkham Estate, Norfolk, England

View of the junction of Pearl and Chatham Streets in New York City, circa 1785. The still existing Shearith Israel's 1682 cemetery is the rectangle in upper right hand corner. What is now Chinatown is at left center; road in upper left through trees is The Bowery; horsecart is at Chatham Square; lower right road is the approach to present Pearl Street; Worth Street is leading off to the left from the horsecart. Courtesy of the New York Historical Society

Illustration of first Shearith Israel synagogue in New York on Mill Street. 1730. By Esther Oppenheim

Drawing of Shearith Israel's 1834 Crosby St. synagogue

Illustration left and above from "An Old Faith in the New World," by David and Tamar DeSola Pool, Columbia University Press, NY 1955

Photo of remaining portion of Shearith Israel's 1682 Cemetery on St. James Place near Chatham Square in New York. Gershom Mendes Seixas burial site is at stone shaft.

Courtesy of American Jewish Historical Society, Newton, MA and New York, NY

6D

SAVANNAH AND MICKVE ISRAEL

Originally, the colony of Carolina consisted of South and North Carolina and Georgia. North Carolina separated in 1729 and Georgia in 1732. The founders of the Georgia colony had the mercantile nature of their enterprise uppermost in their minds. The trustees believed the colony would serve as a British buffer against the Spanish in the south and the French in the west. The Bevis Marks Synagogue in London formed a committee to raise money to support the transportation of Jews to Georgia. One of the well-to-do committee members was Joseph Salvador (Francis Salvador's uncle and father-in-law).[25] Some in the committee felt it would be better if some of the Jews arriving in England from Iberia and central Europe were to leave for the New World "to ease the synagogue of them." During that period of time, the Jewish community tended to take care of their own indigent. Sending some of them to the New World would reduce the number that must be cared for, as there were essentially no governmental social programs, except poorhouses and jails.

Some Sephardic Jews in London also considered purchasing up to 200,000 acres for Jews in South Carolina, or even Nova Scotia. Nothing came of this, although Joseph Salvador bought a large tract in South Carolina in a private purchase.

Five months after James Oglethorpe brought the original colonists to Georgia, the ship *William and Sarah* docked in Savannah in July 1733, carrying forty-two Jewish immigrants, destined for the new Georgia colony. They came without prior approval of either Governor Oglethorpe or the colony's trustees in London. Their voyage was funded through a committee formed by several wealthy members of London's Bevis Marks synagogue. The trip was long and arduous, and included stops for repairs enroute; bitter January weather and gales on the North Atlantic, and a grounding and damage to the ship along the North Carolina coast. The eight Ashkenazim and thirty-four Sephardim would land some six months after they left England.

With them was a Torah (written on deerskin) and a box containing the required surgical items to perform circumcisions, both provided by Bevis Marks. (These historic items can now be seen at the Museum of Mickve Israel in Savannah.) The Jewish passengers presented quite a varied social array – some indigent Ashkenazim asssisted by Bevis Marks, a few fairly well off Ashkenzim (such as the German Sheftalls) and Sephardim. The Bevis Marks committee also planned to send some Ashkenazim to Charleston, but this did not work out. Probably 70 Jews would come to Savannah over the coming year.

Dr. Samuel Nuñez Ribiero, a former court physician in Lisbon, who suffered in the Inquisition, was among the Sephardi group. There was a particular need for Dr. Nuñez because of diseases in the colony, and the fact that the previous physician had died five months earlier. Governor Oglethorpe welcomed the newly arrived doctor with open arms. Dr. Nuñez proved invaluable; not a single person died from the current outbreak after his arrival. At first, over half of the new colonizers were sick. One possibility was that their drinking water came from a very shallow well, so a deeper one was dug.

But Oglethorpe, like the colony's trustees, had not been made aware of the coming of the Jews. He clearly knew the trustees did not welcome these newcomers, as their presence might dissuade others from coming. The Jews on the governor's doorstep raised significant fears in London that Georgia was being overrun by them. Of course, if they had asked for permission, they would not have received it. Despite the trustees' objections, Oglethorpe intervened on the Jews behalf after checking with lawyers in Charleston, who apparently looked at Georgia's charter which excluded only Catholics, slaves and rum, but not Jews. They advised Oglethorpe to let them in.[26]

Oglethorpe in a communication to the trustees praised the Jews' thrift and industry, and mentioned the great service that Dr. Nuñez had performed. The trustees allowed the Jews to stay, and told Oglethorpe to pay Nuñez for his services, but under no circumstances to give land to him or other Jews.

The Bevis Marks congregation worked to increase colonization in Georgia and Carolina, and persisted in trying to get lands for further Jewish colonization, particularly for Jews having little financial resources. It never really worked out.

Not too long after, the Minis family aided the desired increase in colonization by the birth of Philip Minis, believed to be the first non-native child born in Georgia. The circumcision box taken from London was put to use.

The Savannah Jews founded Congregation Mickve Israel (Hope of Israel) in July 1735, established a cemetery and a mikvah in 1738. (Originally, the name commonly used for the congregation was Mickva Israel, which is found up to the 20th century.) Ten more Ashkenazim arrived in Georgia from New York and Charleston in 1738. Religious services apparently started almost immediately in 1733 in what has been described as a crude shack or hut. Torah Scrolls were received in 1733 and 1737 from the Bevis Marks synagogue in London.

Reverend John Bolzius, the minister of a German Protestant group that had just settled in Georgia, thought enough of the kindness of the Jews in giving his people rice soup that he mentioned it in his journal. Some of the Jews were of German origin, so it was a meeting of countrymen with both groups being settlers in quite a strange land. The trustees had hoped to develop a Mediterranean type colony producing wine, olive oil, and for good measure, silk. The charter even called for planting 100 white mulberry trees on each 10 acres cleared. The colony trustees sent a converted Jew, Joseph Ottolenghi, to supervise the silk industry. Silk was eventually exported from Georgia, but was not economically viable without government subsidies. To show the interest of the trustees in silk production, the obverse of the seal of the trustees of Georgia from 1733 to 1752 had a silkworm and cocoon.[27]

The Jews who first landed, and others that followed, mainly by land from other settled colonies, apparently maintained a rift between the Sephardim and the Ashkenazim. There was a minimum of association between the groups.

The same Rev. Bolsius, who was impressed by the Jews' warmth to his group, wrote to a friend in Germany in 1739: "Even the Jews. . .enjoy privileges the same as other colonists. Some call themselves Spanish and Portuguese and others call themselves German. The latter speak High German and differ from the former in their religious services. . .as the former do not seem to take it so particular in regard to the dietary laws and other Jewish ceremonies. They have no synagogue, which is their own fault; the one element hindering the other. The German Jews believe themselves entitled to build a synagogue and are willing to allow the Spanish Jews to use it with them in common, the latter, however, reject any such arrangement and demand the preference for themselves."

The reverend also noted that "German Jews would rather starve" than eat forbidden meats, and the Sephardim were "not so strict."

Despite these problems, the Jews rented a house on Market Square (now Ellis Square) to conduct services.[28] But in a short time (probably due to financial problems) services were moved to the home of Benjamin Sheftall. In 1737 another Torah was received from Benjamin Mendon of London. While Jews were generally accepted by the Christian community, the internal battles and squabbles within the small Jewish community was a factor that tore at the fabric of the group.

By 1740 the economic health of the colony had not improved; the lack of slaves in Georgia's agrarian economy was proving to be too difficult a hurdle to overcome. There were slave economies surrounding them in Charleston, Virginia, the Caribbean and South America, but the trustees forbade it in Georgia. Additionally, many areas were in terrain quite poor for agricultural endeavors.

Also by 1740 the colony had serious territorial defense problems. There were then only about 42 families in Savannah. While Charles II had made huge grants of land on the east coast of North America, the Spanish also claimed an immense chunk of that area of the New World. The English had sought to settle Georgia as both an active colony and a buffer zone against a Spanish invasion of the more northerly colonies.

Locally, the two countries were involved in a major dispute of the land between Charleston and St. Augustine. The Spanish wanted to extend their territory to at least Savannah, eying a further expansion north; while the British thought of an extension south.

Governor Oglethorpe was being harrassed by the Yamassee Indians, allied with the Spanish, who were attacking various islands off the coast of Georgia. To protect his colony the governor blockaded St. Augustine in 1740, hoping to starve the Spanish into submission and possibly capture lands he felt were British. The attack by land and sea failed. Whereupon the Spanish sailed north to attack Jekyll and St. Simons Islands off the coast of Georgia in 1742. They landed over 3,000 soldiers on St. Simons, planning to capture the Georgia colony and eventually (if all went well) the Carolinas.

The Jews in Savannah were highly concerned upon hearing the word that "the Spanish are coming." They feared the Iberian experience would return; the Sephardim, mindful of the Inquisition, were concerned they would be charged with heresy, a "crime" punished by burning. They fled Savannah; by 1741 very few families remained – including the original Minis and Sheftall families. These families had come from Germany and were never involved in forced baptisms as New Christians, and felt they were not under the eye of the Spanish Inquisition.

Some Christians also left for another reason. Due to the colony's ban on slavery, it proved to be very difficult to survive and compete in the agrarian economy where vast areas of the New World were deeply involved with slavery. And to add to the colony's problems, precious little aid was coming from the proprietors in London. The laws and regulations forbidding rum, slavery and restrictions on the ownership of land (and of inheritance of land only to males), led to the downfall and almost to the disintegration of the colony.

Seeing the economic impact of running a non-slave owning colony, the restriction on slavery was lifted in 1750. As a result of the trustees' failure to create an economically viable colony, control was transferred to King George II in 1752.

By 1741 Savannah was nearly a ghost town for Jews (as happened 80 years earlier in New Amsterdam; about 1714 in Charleston, and in 1685 and 1776 in Newport). There was near-dissolution of the Georgia community in 1738.[29] The Jewish community sent the Torah scrolls to New York. The 1741 Journal of the Trustees of Georgia includes, "On the West side of Savannah lies the Township lots of the Jews, all gone to other Colonies except three or four."

Governor Oglethorpe was able to turn back the Spanish in the Battle of Bloody Marsh. In 1746 a few people joined the Jewish community. Bu 1750 there were just 16 Jews in Savannah.

In 1770 the Georgia legislature refused to confirm the title for the expansion of a cemetery owned by Jews, by stating that the owners (Jews) had "imbibed principles entirely repugnant to those of our own (Christian) religion."[30] Three years later the opponents to the Jewish cemetery felt that it would lower land prices. In a *Memorial to Freeholders* they stated that: "no person would choose to buy or rent a House whose Windows looked into a Burial Ground who (those who were dead) might be presumed, from Prejudice of Education to have imbibed Principles entirely repugnant to those of our most holy religion."

In 1774 there was a desire to resume congregational activities and services in the home of Mordecai Sheftall, a son of Benjamin Sheftall, one of the original Jewish colonizers. However, there was another necessary hiatus in the congregation's activities during the Revolutionary War. Mordecai and Levi Sheftall (another son of Benjamin) were active leaders of a local rebel group called the Liberty Boys, who undertook to harass the British. Besides spiking British guns, they stole 500-600 pounds of gunpowder (half the British supply) from the arsenal. Mordecai Sheftall was listed on the British Disqualifying listing as "Chairman of the Rebel Parochial Committee."

Mordecai rose to the position of Commissary General in the Georgia militia, and was Deputy Commissary General to all Continental troops in Georgia and South Carolina, having the rank of colonel, the highest rank of any Jew supporting the patriots in the Revolutionary War. In 1778 Mordecai and his son, Sheftall Sheftall, were captured in trying to escape across a creek.

Mordecai wrote in his diary:

> "...we found it high water; and my son not knowing how to swim, and we, with about one hundred and eighty-six officer and privates being caught...

> it was thought advisable to surrender ourselves prisoners. . ."

Mordecai was considered by one British prison officer "a very great rebel," and was being closely watched during his internment. The Sheftalls were held in the prison-ship, *Nancy,* for one year and released, but told to stay out of Charleston. When they were found traveling to Charleston, they were recaptured and sent to Antigua. After the fall of Savannah and the capture of Mordecai and his son, his wife, Frances, went to Charleston to await them, renting a house on St. Michaels Alley.

She wrote to Mordecai in 1780 describing the attack on Charleston. "During the sige (sic) there was scarce a woman to be seen in the streets. The (canon) balls flew like haile (sic) during the cannonading." And, "We have no less than six Jew children buried since the sige. . ."

In 1780 the father and son were paroled and released in Philadelphia. Mordecai then aided, during the war period, the establishment of the new synagogue building for Mikveh Israel in Philadelphia. On the other hand, his son Sheftall Sheftall, was busy with other matters. Then eighteen, he was commissioned to sail a vessel out of Philadelphia to deliver food to starving American patriot prisoners in Charleston.

After the extended trauma of the war years, Mickve Israel in Savannah was formally reorganized. In 1786 services were resumed in a rented house on Broughton St. Lane, but there was some difficulty, once again, in paying the rent. Instead of abandoning the synagogue's rented space, Mordecai Sheftall (having returned to Savannah), came to the rescue by paying the landlord, Ann Morgan, with merchandise from his general store. The bartered merchandise, in lieu of rent, was listed on the books of the synagogue as, "charge the same to Sedaka (sic) K.K. Mickvah Israel."

For a number of decades Mickve Israel met in various rental spaces or homes with various degrees of congregational successes and failures. By 1791 there was a strong impetus to build a synagogue, but continuing economic problems and a fire caused their plan to be delayed. The synagogue was eventually completed in 1820 -- the first one built in Georgia. The Jewish population was then believed to total just 21 families (94 individuals). Savannah's Jewish population might have grown more from 1790 to 1820 were it not for the enticing bright lights of the city of Charleston sitting just up the road. Levi Sheftall noted in his diary a number of times that the "newcomers to Savannah would soon depart for the attractions of Charleston."[31]

Upon consecrating the building a highly unusual event took place for an orthodox synagogue. A portable organ was used for the first time in a synagogue in the United States. The Torahs were carried through the streets to the new synagogue. Specific psalms were selected for the occasion and sung accompanied by the organ, during the seven times the Torahs were carried around the Tabah (central reading stand).[32] The organ was played by the director of Savannah's Independent Presbyterian Church. (It is not known whether the organ was used in regular services.)

The building was destroyed in a fire in 1829. A brick synagogue was completed by 1838 and dedicated by Rabbi Isaac Leeser of Philadelphia in 1841. With the arrival of many Ashkenazim the building proved to be too small, and the present Gothic revival synagogue was dedicated in 1878 on Gordon Street, off Monterey Square. The *Savannah Recorder* noted: "The synagogue is one of the most tasty and elegant in the south, and surpasses in beauty many in larger cities."

The Savannah move to Reform Judaism was started in 1868, and was gradually instituted by omitting the second days of festivals, and permanently by introducing musical accompaniment and a choir. Reverend Isaac P. Mendes, who served Mickve Israel from 1877 to 1904, tried to staunch the congregation's move towards reform. He slowed it, saying at least once that "he was opposed to change," and tried to instill greater observance of the Sabbath. But the members apparently preferred a more liberal attitude in both ritual and observance. The rabbi could not stop the tide of change. In February 1880 a chupah (wedding canopy) was made optional, and so, too, were skullcaps towards the end of the century.

Reform Judaism was fully in place, so in 1904 Mickve Israel joined the Union of American Hebrew Congregations (now the Union for Reform Judaism), the association of synagogues practicing Reform Judaism.

It is difficult not to make a final mention of Sheftall Sheftall, who was captured (with his father) during the Revolutionary War. He was so caught up in the war's fervor that he refused, up to his death in 1848, to change his style of clothes. He kept wearing knickerbocker pants and three cornered hats, and was very proud of his dated outfits. He gently disregarded the not so gentle needling by onlookers, who were by then calling him "Cocked Hat Sheftall."

6E

JEWISH COMMUNITY OF PHILADELPHIA AND MIKVEH ISRAEL

Pennsylvania's first constitution in 1682 did require a belief in Christianity. Article 34 of the document reads in part: "...all members elected to serve in provincial Council and General Assembly, and all that have right to elect such members, shall be such as to possess faith in Jesus Christ..."

By 1706 the law placed civic restrictions on those who did not profess faith in the Trinity, or acknowledge the divine inspiration of the New Testament. As the Jewish community slowly started to develop, little attention was apparently paid to the letter of the law. The Protestant legislature seemed focused on encumbering Catholics, but both Catholics and Jews were impacted in that cemeteries and other religious properties could not be directly owned if they did not belong to the "proper" religious sect. Someone would have to hold it in their name.

There were barely any Jews around in 1706 to worry about such laws. Fort Christiana was built by the Swedish near Wilmington, Delaware, as part of New Sweden, a colony that lasted from 1638 to 1655. Sweden was trying to increase their foreign trade by emulating the British and Dutch models, but it didn't work out. Peter Stuyvesant had little difficulty in capturing the area and making it part of New Netherlands, which now encompassed the Delaware River to Albany, New York, and down the Hudson River to Manhattan. To underscore the complexity of various land grabs at that time, Stuyvesant delayed occupying New Sweden, because Sweden was then supporting the Dutch in ongoing wars in Europe.

The first Jewish settlers came to Pennsylvania in the early 1700s, but there is little notice of an active Jewish community until about 1730. Most of them were of German background. As commerce in the colony increased in the 1730s and 1740s, Jews (including some wealthy families involved in shipping) arrived from New York. By this time Philadelphia was as large, or larger, than New York. Other small communities of Jews were in Easton, Reading and Lancaster, which were important in the frontier fur trade. A cemetery was purchased in Philadelphia about 1738, and another established in Lancaster. And in Philadelphia services were held in the mid-1740s, and by the 1750s they took place in a rented room on Sterling Alley.

Nathan Levy, the son of a major New York merchant, did much to support the small Jewish community in Philadelphia. He donated a cemetery to the community that he had privately purchased for his family, and significantly supported Shearith Israel Synagogue in New York. However, the cemetery wall was used for target practice in 1751, and an ad was put in the *Pennsylvania Gazette* asking "unthinking people" to "forbear firing against the said wall" and damaging tombstones.

There is no record if there were continuing regular services starting in the 1740s. A formal congregation was not formed at that time. As Edwin Wolf says in *The History of the Jews of Philadelphia,* they joined in worship, augmented by Jews from Lancaster and solitary Jews from nearby towns. However, he states, "they did not establish a congregation in any formal sense. Mikveh Israel in time grew out of this loose association, but its regular life as a congregation did not begin until some decades later. The early Philadelphia minyan (prayer group) had no name, no rules or constitution and no officers or clerical leader."[33]

There was little movement towards actually constructing a synagogue in Philadelphia until about 1761, when a letter from Jacob Henry of New York to Bernard Gratz in Philadelphia commented on talk of erecting a building. Henry was convinced that this news meant: "Eternity is nigh at hand" and that the service would be Quaker -- meaning no service at all.[34] Quakers would meet silently until someone was moved to say something spiritual to the gathering—with no prayers, sermons or structured service.

Records exist that a Torah was borrowed by the Pennsylvania Jews from New York in 1761. It is believed that the Torah was used in Philadelphia, although there is an outside possibility that the Torah was for Lancaster, Pennsylvania, inasmuch as that city had a very small Jewish community holding services in a house synagogue.

There appears to have been serious internal squabbles that delayed the formation of a cohesive religious community. As noted earlier under the New York section, Gershom Mendes Seixas of Shearith Israel came to Philadelphia from Stamford, Connecticut in 1780. He and other patriots had abandoned New York during the Revolutionary War when the British initially entered Long Island in 1776.

Philadelphia may have had 300 Jews out of a population of 35,000 (about 0.85%) just before the Revolutionary War. By the 1780s Philadelphians showed active interest in erecting a synagogue. And as a result of British activities, there were many important out-of-towners who were movers and motivators in their own cities, including Gershom Mendes Seixas, who was always a motivator and catalyst for action. Additionally, Isaac DaCosta, one of the founding members of KKBE in Charleston, was in Philadelphia in 1781, as was Abraham Mendes Seixas, Gershom's brother. The war brought them together for a short period. Abraham Seixas' prayer book recorded that he was "banish'd from Chas Town as disaffected to British Govt and arrived in Philada (sic) 29th May 1782."

In March 1782 Isaac DaCosta was chairman of a group raising funds for the building. DaCosta and his son, and a number of others had left Charleston for Philadelphia. Some ten Jews from Charleston were listed as members of Mikveh Israel around this time. They may all have left Charleston for the same reason – the required Loyalty Oath of 1778 decreed either swearing allegiance to British South Carolina or leaving the state, and the confiscation of their property.[35] There was a desire for a synagogue, and these and a number of other out-of-towners started to move the process along.

There were also Jews from New York and Savannah, ready to aid Seixas and the Philadelphians. The newcomers had assumed control of the project.

Land was purchased for the synagogue on Sterling Alley in 1782, but later, a lot was chosen on Cherry Alley, and the original property was sold. At the first meeting of the reorganized congregation that year the building of a synagogue was actively discussed. One question was *"whether the Old Building on the Lot Bought for the use of the Synagogue should be repaired first in order to (be) a place of worship or should we agree to build a New One? And on examination of the difft (different) Estimates of the Repairs. . .and finding that a New Buildg would not cost much more than the repairs. . ."* they resolved that *"a New Synagogue be built."* Among the signatories were Isaac Da Costa, Chairman (from Charleston), Gershom Seixas (from New York), Mordacai Sheftall (from Savannah and Charleston) and Haym Salomon (from New York and Philadelphia. It became a true national effort with the best hearts and minds involved. Salomon had previously pledged his fortune in support of the Revolution. James Madison said of Salomon, "I have for some time. . .been a pensioner on the favor of Haym Salomon, a Jew Broker."

The combination of Philadelphian Jews and the temporary, but highly qualified transients from other colonial cities, hastened the construction of the new synagogue and a new mikvah. Dedication of Mikveh Israel took place on Sept. 13, 1782. Invitations were sent to the Governor and the Supreme Executive Council. Haym Levy of New York, who contributed the third largest amount, £75, had the honor of opening the Ark at the opening ceremonies. He was also an official of Shearith Israel in New York.

A letter sent to the political leaders in Philadelphia included this paragraph: *"The Congregation of Mikveh Israel (Israelites) in this city, have erected a place of publick worship which they intend to consecrate to the service of Almighty God, tomorrow afternoon."* It further stated that they will deem themselves highly honored by the presence of the Governor and other high-level officials in the synagogue *"whenever they judge proper to favour them."* The doors would be *"open'd at three and the service continue 'till seven."*[36]

The dedication of this first permanent synagogue followed Orthodox Sephardic tradition. Gershom Seixas served as hazzan at Mikveh Israel until 1784, and may have stayed longer, except that his congregation in New York was most fervently pressing for his return. After the war most returned to their home cities (as did Seixas and DaCosta). But not all – some enjoyed Philadelphia's ambiance and remained.

Toward the end of their activities in Philadelphia, Seixas, Barnard Gratz and Haym Salomon framed a petition, asking that the Pennsylvania Constitution be revised, and that the requirement to declare upon taking public office that the New Testament was of divine inspiration, be removed. While nothing came of the request regarding the Pennsylvania Constitution, just four years later the Federal Constitution, drafted in the same city, had the "no religious test" clause.

It was quickly determined – and not surprisingly – that there were inadequate funds for operations and maintenance of the new synagogue. This was also the case in Newport after the construction of their beautiful synagogue. In dire need of money, Mikveh Israel asked both Jews and non-Jews for support.

With inadequate funds coming in, the synagogue took an entirely different direction – a lottery. Mikveh Israel asked the General Assembly for permission to run a lottery.[37] In 1788 the synagogue clearly, and emphatically, stated their need for funds to pay obligations and "other debts that is now not only pressingly claim'd but a Judgement will actually be obtained against their house of worship which must be sold unless they are speedily enabled to pay a sum of about £800."[38]

A 1788 subscription list for funds shows many non-Jewish supporters, such as Benjamin Franklin, £5, Wm. Bradford, £3, (an important patriot and anti-British publisher) and David Rittenhouse, £2, (later director of the U.S. mint). The document's preamble states that "the remaining few of their Religion here burthen'd (sic) with a considerable charge from so great an Undertaking." But the amount raised did not solve their financial problems.

Many churches in Philadelphia and the Christ Church steeple had been built or improved by using lotteries. While they waited for approval, the city of Philadelphia itself was engaged in aiding the building of a city hall through a lottery.

Approval by the General Assembly for Mikveh Israel's lottery was received in April 1790, and included as one of the sales agents was Isaac Moses, selling tickets from his Wall Street offices.

The advertising for the lottery stated, in part:

> ". . .while for the small sum of two dollars and one-half, which they do venture in this, they have the chance of drawing a prize of 1000 dollars, or even 1400 dollars, besides the satisfaction of having contributed to an object so pious and meritorious."

The state, as was normal, lent two lottery wheels for the drawing on October 19, 1790. Their goal was to raise £300 to "extricate their House of Worship from its present incumbrances." Apparently the lottery resolved the synagogue's financial problems -- but only temporarily. The synagogue, clearly in financial trouble again, announced on Rosh Hashanah in 1792, that those Jews who received benefits of the synagogue (such as kosher meat; services of a mohel; and birth, marriage and burial rites), and who did not financially support the congregation:

> "shall be deemed as not belonging to our society either in public or in private. . .; and in case of Death of themselves or any of their family residing within their dwelling they shall not be entitled to the aid or the attendance usual on such occasions from any person belonging to the congregation."

Low attendance and violations of the rules of the Sabbath were also problems. Three attempts were made to put a rule in the constitution, that those not keeping the Sabbath would be subject to expulsion. It was turned down three times. Intermarriage was another concern.

By 1795 there were many newcomers to Philadelphia who were not satisfied or comfortable with the Sephardic minhag or with Mikveh Israel. These were mainly Ashkenazi Polish, German and Dutch Jews. The exact steps followed in the formation of the next synagogue, Rodeph Shalom, are not clear. The minutes of Mikveh Israel do not hint of a split or of dissension. But some Jews wanted an alternative congregation – an Orthodox Ashkenazi synagogue that was formed by the German Hebrew Society. A mikvah was established in 1796; a deed for a cemetery in 1801, and in 1802 a German synagogue, Rodeph Shalom was dedicated. Philadelphia became the first city to have two permanent synagogues.

(Charleston, South Carolina underwent a period of

conflict within Kahal Kadosh Beth Elohim about 1786, which caused an apparent split and the formation of two synagogues for a period probably no longer than five years.)

Rodeph Shalom's first constitution was written in Yiddish, with an English translation. And with two synagogues in town, Mikveh Israel quickly found that they had to try to restrict "wandering" between synagogues. In 1810 their constitution forbade any of their members attending other minyans, or other congregations.

One more story is worth telling about early Philadelphia. It's the ironic history of the Liberty Bell's voyage to the U.S. after being cast in London. William Penn had restricted the rights of Jews to vote and to hold office in Pennsylvania. What was to be named the Liberty Bell years later was brought here in 1751 on ships owned by the Jewish firm of Levy and Franks. It was to commemorate the 50th anniversary of William Penn's Charter of Liberties. However, not all liberties were available to Levy and Franks. They were excluded from voting, as were all other Jews, as they didn't profess belief in Jesus Christ. Again we found the early Jews persevering along the long road to full civic equality.

7A

CHARLESTON, JOHN LOCKE AND THE COLONY OF CAROLINA

Charles II granted a charter to eight Lord Proprietors to start a colony in North America. He gave them territory that stretched from about the present Florida-Georgia border to just south of Virginia, and in one grand sweep westward, to the "South Seas." About 1669 a Federal Constitution for that planned colony (originally South Carolina, North Carolina and Georgia) was written in London by John Locke, the English philosopher, and Lord Anthony Ashley Cooper (the First Earl of Shaftesbury). This document and its succeeding drafts would never be approved by the colony as it proposed a rather cumbersome, almost feudal social structure. At the same time it also set a surprisingly forward-looking tone of religious tolerance that would take hold and make Carolina one of the most welcoming colonies for the practice of religion. The proposals established and granted religious freedom and opportunities to the new immigrants rarely available elsewhere.

The promotional literature to attract settlers to this vast area described a paradise for those who would but cross the Atlantic. The streets were certainly not paved in gold *(they were not paved at all)*, but the advertisements trying to lure women to Carolina read for example: "If any maid or single women have a desire to go over, they will think themselves in the Golden Age – for if they be but civil, and under 50 years of age, some honest man will purchase them for wives."[1]

An *Account of the Province of Carolina* stated the "ayr" (air) of Charles Town "gives strong appetite and Quick Digestion…men finding themselves more lightsome. ..and Women are very Fruitful and the Children have fresh Sanguine Complexions."

Clearly, some of the boosters let their prose get out of hand. Shortly after 1680 a pamphlet pushing for a proposed colony south of Savannah (which never happened) stated that "Carolina, and especially its Southern Bounds, is the most amiable Country in the Universe, that Nature has not bless'd the World with any Tract, which can be preferable to it, that Paradise, with all her Virgin Beauties may be modestly suppos'd at most but equal to its Native Excellences."[2] Who could top that!

Immigrants to the planned colony would certainly risk dangers. Besides the long and dangerous voyage, these included disease; possible starvation from years of proof crops; not so friendly neighbors such as the aggressive and land-hungry Spanish to the south and the French to the west; Indians who were supporting whoever best served their purposes while trying to defend their territory; and off-shore, cut-throat pirates who were doing their own thing. A new colony was a gamble that there would be new and better opportunities for a better life.

Other colonists were hoping to distance themselves from old-world problems, hoping that things, no matter how difficult, would be better across the Atlantic. The eight Lords Proprietors of the colony on the other hand were gambling on a hoped for money-making enterprise. These aristocrats had been given very large land holdings in the colony as political patronage, or as payoff for debts (financial or political) owed them by the monarchy. Many proprietors would never visit the colony, desiring an arms-length financial investment, gaining rewards but choosing not to invest too much of their own capital in this chancy foreign enterprise. In fact, their reluctance to adequately fund the colony during its early critical period would cause great problems for the settlers.

To initiate the colony, three ships, *Carolina, Port Royal* and *Albermarle,* left England for Carolina in August 1669 under the command of Joseph West. We do know that the voyage certainly was not an easy one, the passengers proving their mettle even before stepping ashore in Carolina. Their first stop was in Kinsale, Ireland where they hoped to add some brave souls to their numbers before the crossing. But many travelers re-assessed their imminent foreign adventure, so there were more defectors than new volunteers.

They then set sail for the active and crowded British colony of Barbados, again anticipating that that island would bring fresh colonists onboard. Things were going fairly well with the ships reaching the Caribbean island in October. However, the *Albermarle* was unfortunately wrecked in a storm in Barbados. At that point Sir John Yeamans, a wealthy planter in Barbados, was given a commission that allowed him to designate himself or another as governor of the new colony.[3] Yeamans leased a sloop in Barbados as a replacement for the *Albermarle,* and then set sail for Carolina.

Things then really started to go awry. The newly acquired sloop was blown in violent storms all the way to Virginia, the *Port Royal* was wrecked in the Bahamas, and the *Carolina* with Yeamans aboard finally found safe haven in Bermuda. At that point Yeamans (who would later prove to be shrewd, unprincipled and self-serving) reassessed his priorities. In a letter to the colony's proprietors in London he told his version of what happened, stating that ". . .how by the hand of God through the violence of stormes and contrary winds your Fleete became dispersed . . .and with much difficulty had attained the Harbour of Burmoodoes. . ." He noted that the ships needed refitting to continue the voyage, but it would have been too long a period for him to stay around, and he had to return to Barbados to take care of his many business affairs on that island. By the commission that had been given to him he "...substituted Col. Wm. Sayles....although a man of noe great sufficiency yet the ablest I could then meete with..." as the new governor of the colony of Carolina.[4]

Another observer, at a later date, commented in a very similar vein that Sayles, a former governor of Bermuda, who would become the first governor of the colony, was "...very anchant... and very feble...He is one of the onfittest men in the world...for being governor."[5] Sayles was near eighty at the time.

With such stirring words the colony of Carolina set up its first community in Port Royal, when the appropriately named ship *Carolina* finally landed in April 1670 after a seven month trip. The landing site was just seven miles north of present day Charleston and close to where the Synagogue Emanu-El is now located. The sloop that had been blown to Virginia arrived some two months later after traveling too far south to Georgia, and then returning to the new colony. Sayles remained governor to March 1671.

By that year newly arrived colonists must have been homesick for their mother country, because all shipmasters were required to post bonds that they would not transport inhabitants out of the colony without special licenses. The following year the population was about 400, having quadrupled since the landing, mainly through aggressive recruitment in Barbados, which had become a very crowded island. The early 1670s were difficult for the colony due to drought and the lack of cheap labor. Slaves did not arrive in larger numbers until the introduction of rice in the 1690s.

THE PHILOSOPHY OF JOHN LOCKE AND HIS IMPACT ON CAROLINA

John Locke drafted the Fundamental Constitution of Carolina in 1669 at the request of Lord Anthony Ashley

Cooper. Locke, who was 37, was advisor, secretary and physician to Cooper, and is believed to be the primary author of the Fundamental Constitution for the colony. Locke had been a lecturer in Greek and philosophy at Christ Church College, and studied medicine as well. The colony chose never to formally adopt the constitution despite a very long and active effort by Cooper and others to get its adoption. While I will quote items from the first draft of 1669, there were at least five drafts over the years, the last being as late as 1698. Despite failure in getting the constitution adopted, the document proved to be most significant in that Locke's (and Cooper's) farsighted thoughts regarding religious freedom and tolerance became firmly established in this British colony.

Locke believed that human beings were equal and independent, and that no one had the right to harm another's "life, health, liberty or possessions." He believed that allowing freedom of conscience and the pursuit of happiness and pleasure by the individual would, in the long run, be good for the general community. He developed the concepts of "checks and balances" within a governmental structure. (Some of these thoughts and words are very similar to those found in the United States Constitution written some 100 years later.) While Locke would at a later date write important essays on religious freedom and tolerance, he really did not accept atheism or Roman Catholicism, both of which he believed should be legislated against as being inimical to the state's well being.

The draft constitution for Carolina contained some of the most progressive philosophies regarding religious freedom and tolerance to be found in the 17th century:

> "Noe p'rson shall use any reproachfull revileing or abusive language against ye religion of any church or profession. . ." as it is ". . .the certain way of disturbing ye publick peace and of hindering ye conversion of any to ye truth by ingageing them in quarrills

> an animosities. . .", and amazingly for that time,
> "No person whatsoever shall disturbe, molest or p'rsecute another for his speculative opinions in religion or his way of worship."[6]

At the same time the draft constitution maintained a hierarchical landed-class social structure, certainly not a democracy as we understand it, but it did allow a large measure of individual freedom, including a mandated secret ballot. As Lord Ashley Cooper stated: ". . .noe bodys power, noe not any of the proprietors themselves. . .is soe great as to be able to hurt the meanest man in the Country."

Locke stated it was unreasonable to keep out new settlers who might have religious opinions differing from the Anglican Church, and that "If we allow Jews to have private houses and dwellings among us, why should we not allow them to have synagogues."[7] It included "ye liberty" to "heathens, Jues (sic) and other dissenters." There are also paragraphs mentioning those that are "utter strangers to Christianity, whose idolatry, ignorance or mistake gives us noe right to expel them, or use them ill, and those from other parts. . .will unavoydably be of diffrent opinions concerning matters of religion. . ."

And that the "heathens, Jues, and other dissenters may not be scared and kept at a distance from it, but by having an opportunity of acquainting themselves with ye truth and reasonableness of its doctrines. . .may by good usage and perswasion and all those convincing methods of gentleness and meekness. . . .be wone over to embrace. . . and receive ye truth. Therefor any seaven or more persons agreeing in any religion shall constitute a church or profession to w(hi)ch they shall give it some name to distinguish it from others."[8] And all that was necessary is that they "acknowledge a God, and that God is publicly and solemly worshipped."

There is a barely hidden, underlying thought within

the quote above. To Locke, "ye truth" was Protestantism – that those professing other religions will on viewing the Protestant religion would, on their own, see the value of Protestantism. In an almost unique and refreshing idea for the times the means and desire to "see the light" was in the *sole* control of the dissenters. No torture, and no flames to help "reveal" the truth. This concept of tolerance was not solely Locke's, but was supported by Ashley Cooper, and clearly spelled out in a letter from Cooper to Governor Sayles in 1671. On discussing an allotment of land and salary to a preacher, he states:

"... wee give neither him nor you Authority to compel any one in matters of Religion having in our Federal Constitution granted a freedom in that pointe which we resolve to keep inviolable." He signed the letter "Ashley."[9]

Carolina proved to be a most hospitable area for Jews and other dissenters. Jews could from the start practice their religion openly, could own businesses and property. As a result Charleston had by 1810 the largest number of Jews of any city in the country.

Gaining civic equality for Jews, even in Carolina of the 1700s, was an uphill climb – but significantly less so than in many of the other colonies. People were much more concerned with day-to-day livelihood and family issues, and the vitriolic hatred towards Jews that was endemic in much of the world was not present on their doorstep. There was a realistic outlook that gains in social areas take time, and time is available when not under the gun or torch. These new immigrants made the most of the available economic opportunities and were surely most grateful for the peace and safety from violence by their neighbors, which was such a continuing part of the European experience. Economic and religious tolerance was amazing for its day, and allowed the Jewish community to develop slowly.

Colonial life for the average person was hard. But with the hardships came a chance to make a new and, hopefully, better life and to many of the Jews (and there were but a handful at the start) it was a hard but golden opportunity, in a new and amazingly tolerant colony. And much of the basis for the tolerance can be traced to the Constitution, a remarkable, strange document that was never formally approved, but contained concepts that became an integral part of the colony's culture. The Jews were able to live full fruitful lives.

Tolerance in many other British colonies may have been due to their realistic concerns in maintaining economic well being. Spanish colonies stifled religious freedom where "blood purity" was a prime concern. A number of their colonies were driven into the ground economically through their single-minded focus on religious purity and uniformity, as well as by shipping much of their production and wealth to the home country. The British had seen the advantages that Jews brought to existing Dutch colonies. Jews were viewed as good colonizers who were industrious settlers who fostered economic well being and opportunities, and were known as generally being supportive of the government in power.

There was the successful but short-lived Dutch colony in Pernambuco, Brazil from 1630 to 1654. Prior to the formation of Carolina, the British actually welcomed Jews to Jamaica, particularly after the Jews aided the British in capturing that island from Spain in 1655. And the British actively sought Jews in Surinam (in NE South America) in 1665. The British government even granted formal assurances of their safety. This was but five years before the founding of Carolina. These feelings regarding Jewish settlers possibly carried over and played a part in creating governmental tolerance towards Jewish settlers in Carolina.

While Locke's forward-looking tolerant concepts regarding religious activities and political participation were clearly defined in the constitution, he also tried to establish a feudal and aristocratic based social order in the colony of

Carolina. Baronies and nobles known as Landgraves were to be the major landowners, with lesser landowners to be called Caciques, and common field laborers or serfs to be called Leetman. These serfs were to be bound to their owners with no chance for the lower echelons to advance. The draft constitution stated:

> "...nor shall any leetman or leetwoman have liberty to goe from the land of his particular lord & live anywhere else without licences obtain'd from his said lord under hand and seale... All children of leetman shall be leetman, & so to all generations, and they cannot ...live anywhere else without licences obtained from his said lord..."[10]

The ideas within the drafts seemed to be pulling in two directions: highly tolerant religious concepts and a proposed repressive social order for many except the wealthy aristocratic class. There were also restrictive rules on property acquisition and inheritance. While this arrangement certainly seems strange in our times, it was an attempt to assure that the landed class and nobility would retain control of the colony, and while there would be an elected assembly, the assembly's actions would be subject to control by the aristocracy. It should be remembered that the social order in England at that time essentially established three social levels – royalty, titled aristocrats and commoners.

The draft also included items regarding slaves: "Every freeman of Carolina shall have absolute power and authority over his Negro slaves of what opinion or religion soevr."

Locke wrote that religion "...ought to alter nothing in any mans civil estate or right."

He was addressing the question of whether slaves who were Christian would remain slaves under other Christians, believing that slaves could "...be of what church any of them shall think best..." but that "..noe slave shall hereby be exempted from that civill dominion his mastr hath ovr him, but be in all other things ye same state and condicon he was in before." By the end of the 1690s the attempt to implement the Federal Constitution was abandoned by the Lord Proprietors, a recognition that the colonists would not implement these radical social ideas.

In 1675 Ashley Cooper opposed Charles II's efforts to improve the status of Roman Catholics in Great Britain. Cooper was eventually charged with treason, a capital crime, but the indictment failed. To preserve his head he quickly departed for Holland, where he died in 1713.

The first Jew known to have been in Charles Town was a Spanish-speaking translator brought in by Governor Archdale in 1695. His name is unknown, but Governor Archdale noted in his papers that there was a "Jew for an Interpreter" This translator was involved with a question dealing with the capture of four Spanish-speaking Indians (three men and one women). On determining they were Roman Catholics the Indians were returned to the Spaniards in St. Augustine.

That Jews were not in Charles Town at an earlier date seems unusual, considering the amazing mobility of both Sephardim and Ashkenazim at that time. Jews were in New York since 1654, Newport since 1658, Barbados since the lates 1620s, Curaçao since 1651 and Amsterdam since 1595. It almost begs credibility that it took Jews some 25 years after the settlement of Charles Town in 1670 for them to appear in this religiously tolerant community.

In 1697 sixty eight people (four of whom were Jews) were made citizens of the colony when an act was passed "making aliens free" and granting "liberty of conscience to all Protestants". The four Jews were each described as "an alien of ye Jewish Nation."[11] Jews were in fact included or treated as if they were Protestants in many instances. Jews and Huguenots (French Protestants) among others, were allowed to vote for members of the Assembly in 1703.

SOME OPPOSITION TO RELIGIOUS TOLERANCE AND CIVIC INCLUSION

In the mid to late 1680s, prior to the first known Jew coming to Charles Town, there were serious efforts by a group of Anglicans from Barbados – called the Goose Creek men – to restrict the voting rights of dissidents and to only grant the vote to members of the Anglican Church. They also opposed the adoption of the proposed constitution.

In 1692 the Anglican clergy attempted to restrict other ministers from performing marriages, claiming that marriages performed by Huguenot ministers, for example, were illegal and that children from that union were illegitimate. A protest to the proprietors resulted in the governor being told that all Protestants enjoyed "liberty of conscience" and the Assembly then gave religious freedom to all Christians except Roman Catholics. But by April 1702 an act was passed allowing Roman Catholics to vote, and despite the high animosity between Protestant and Catholics that act was never repealed. Yet, there were loud complaints to London about Jews and others voting, and in the world of the east coast colonies such acts of civic inclusion and religious toleration in the early 1700s were extremely unusual.

Letters of protest regarding voting by dissidents and non-Christians were sent to Queen Anne. Lord Granville, a proprietor of the colony, also felt that, "If a man holds a false and illegal religion he cannot be fit to sit in Parliament and legislate for people who know the truth." He resolved to stop the people who were now ruling (or "ruining" as he felt) the colony. Others wrote to London saying, "...at this last Election, Jews, Strangers, Sailors, Servants, Negroes and almost every French man. . .came down to elect and their votes were taken. . ."

The Assembly went about trying to "correct" this problem – as they saw it – of Jews and other dissidents possibly being in the legislature. A resolution in the Charles

Town Assembly in May 1704 would have required all Assembly members to "take the oaths and conform to the religious worship of the Church of England and receive the Sacrament of the Lord's Supper according to the rights of said church."

The major opponent to this "Church Act" was Reverend Edward Marston of St. Phillip's Church, who respected the right of the dissenters. This caused the proponents of the "Act" much anguish; they certainly did not expect opposition from that source. Queen Anne, in response to what was going on, stated through her law officers that such acts were not "...consonant to reason, and being repugnant to the laws of England..." the Queen "might therfor declare these laws null and void and require the Proprietors and Assembly of the Province to abrogate them."[12] The Queen then did declare the "Act" null and void and sent this decision to Charles Town.

The Queen's response was not taken well by the Assembly. Such ideas as formally recognizing and supporting one religion (such as the Anglican Church in this case) was most common in colonial America. The favoring of one religion over another by the state legislatures lasted in some colonies well into the 19th century.

The failed draft constitution had stated that the colony:

> "acknowledges a God and that God is publicly and solemnly worshipped," and where called to be a witness "...that every church or profession shall in theire termes of com'union sett downe ye externall way wherby they witness a truth as in ye presence of God, whether it be by laying hands on or kissing ye Bible as in ye Protestant or Papist churches, or by holding up ye hand or any other sensible way."

Liberty of conscience was a part of this constitution. There were in Charles Town by 1700 a broad array of religions – Anglicans, Scotch and English Presbyterians, New England Congregationalists, Quakers, Baptists, Huguenots and Jews among others. These religious differences were a lesser issue until James Moore, an Anglican, was elected governor, and by 1704 he sought to establish the Anglican Church as the colony's church. With his backing it didn't take the Assembly long to start disassembling those thoughts and words about "liberty of conscience." The Assembly started putting specific conditions based on religion, and what they considered were 'dissenting' religions. With a very small majority a bill passed that excluded any but Church of England believers from the legislature, and a few months later had that church supported by general tax revenue. The text explaining why the Church was being made the state religion included:

> "...It hath been found by experience that the admitting of persons of different religious persuasions hath often caused great contentions and animosities in this Province and hath very much obstructed the public business."

This legislation of 1704 was openly opposed by many in the community and it was repealed in 1706, only to be superceded by another act that imposed once again the role of the Anglican Church as the colony's church. By then an Establishment Act laid out boundaries for ten Church of England parishes, and specified the amount of tax support for church maintenance, and for clergy salaries.[13]

The legislature, now being on a roll, decided in 1710 to open a free school (believed to be the first in the colonies) to teach arts, sciences and the principles of Christianity. They were given a house, land and salary as long as the teacher was a member of the Church of England. Everything was ready, but for some reason the school did not get started until 1722. In 1721 a report by the Anglican clergy stated that the church was: "daily encreasing (sic)..."

and that other sects would in another generation be "near Extinct." Clearly, all European religious conflicts were not washed away during the crossing of the Atlantic.

Many factions within the population were now putting forward agendas that included: trying to strengthen the position of the Church of England; groups that opposed or supported the proprietors; groups that wanted closer or more distant ties with the Indians, and groups that did or did not want to bring black and Indian slaves into the colony. Additionally, there were moves to rid the colony of the governance by the Lord Proprietors, and this did happen in 1720 with the establishment of Carolina as a Crown colony.

Despite all this factionalism and the legislative activity by Church of England supporters, Charleston was still most welcoming to the open practice of religion, and was still a most welcoming place for the Jews. Jews had almost no civic handicaps that really impacted their lives,and did serve in some municipal positions. By the early 1700s there may have been just enough Jews to hold the prayer services that required a minimum of 10 men. The fact that by 1715, Mordecai Nathan and Simon Valentine, coming to Charleston from New York, established a business of shipping kosher beef out of Charleston indicates that there was some sort of viable Jewish community.[14] However, the number of Jews (and businesses) in Charleston would, for reasons not fully understood, remain static from 1715 to 1730. This formerly active and mainly Sephardic community was in trouble.

Current data leaves us to believe that the Jewish population of Charleston was stationary for at least twenty years prior to 1726. However, a recovery started slowly in the 1730s. The Jews were generally Sephardim from London, the Caribbean, Amsterdam and other American colonies. By the 1740s the town had some 7,000 inhabitants, the fourth largest city in the colonies. And there were some

12-15 Jewish families, half of which were Sephardim, and there were thoughts of forming a congregation. The increase in the Jewish population may have resulted from many leaving Savannah and coming to Charleston, due to both Georgia's economic difficulties,as well as the Spaniards trying to capture Georgia from the British. Additionally, the English-Spanish, and the English-French Wars of the 1740s apparently bolstered the economy of Charleston by increasing trade out of the port. Charleston was starting to grow. More ships were registered in Charleston; shippers found that Charleston was an excellent harbor for the distribution of goods to the South.

The figure that seems to be in general consensus is that there were some 1,500-2,000 Jews in the United States at the time of the Revolutionary War. That the Jews were able to defend their rights, establish congregations and start to build synagogues, despite their minimal population is nothing short of startling. Resistance to Roman Catholicism had been a continuing fact in the normally religiously tolerant Charleston. And South Carolina was one of the few states that rapidly abolished all religious tests for holding office or voting, and its 1790 constitution allowed all its citizens "the free exercise and enjoyment of religious profession and worship, without discrimination of preferences," even allowing for the incorporation of religious organizations.

7B

CHARLESTON AND KAHAL KADOSH BETH ELOHIM 1749-1838

In September 1749 Kahal Kadosh Beth Elohim (Holy Congregation House of God – KKBE) was established with Moses Cohen selected as "Chief Rabbi" or Chacham (literally translated as *Learned One*) and Isaac DaCosta as hazzan. Cohen did not have "smichah," the recognized education or the formal ordination to become a rabbi. The congregants adopted the Sephardic (Spanish/Portuguese) liturgy. (There were no advanced Jewish educational systems in the colonies to formally teach Jewish Law and the practices of the religion – and there would not be one for another 120 years.) And they would not lay a cornerstone for their first synagogue for another 43 years.

The first hazzan (or reader) was Isaac DaCosta whose family came from Portugal through London. The Coming Street cemetery property was acquired from DaCosta in 1764, making it the oldest Jewish cemetery now in the south. The congregation was meeting for services on State Street (formerly Union Street) but moved to Hasell Street in 1775, to the second floor of a large house near the site of the current synagogue. Services were strictly Orthodox, using the Sephardic prayer ritual, closely following those of the Bevis Marks Synagogue in London, and the great Portuguese synagogue in Amsterdam.

The Jewish community grew slowly during this period. Most participated in the economic growth of the area, particularly as small shopkeepers. They were also involved in coastal and international trade. There were some active business linkages with Jews in other major colonial cities. And there were no restrictions establishing companies involving both Jews and non-Jews.

Charles Town was growing and was becoming one of the most important ports in the colonies. The shipping industry was primarily involved in the transportation of agricultural products – rice, indigo (a plant-based dye used in the textile trade of the time), and somewhat later, cotton.

As a clear indication of the British governor's holding commerce above religious doctrine, he appointed Moses Lindo, a Jew from London who emigrated in 1756, to bolster the indigo trade in the colony, which was introduced into the Carolinas by Eliza Lucas, the future wife of Chief Justice Charles Pinkney. Despite her agricultural knowledge, there was a need to improve the quality of the indigo crop. Liquid was extracted from the plant and after proper processing, it was turned into a strong, permanent blue dye.

Moses Lindo was very experienced in indigo grading and production, and highly thought of in London. He was appointed South Carolina's Surveyor and Inspector-General of Indigo, Dyes and Drugs in 1762, a position he held for 10 years, and would foster a major increase in the importance of indigo in the colony's economy. Specifically, Lindo saw the need to improve the quality and quantity of the crop so that it would be accepted in the competitive market place and would receive a good price by the English textile industry. Some of the major producers were France, Jamaica and India.

In the ten years Lindo was involved a much higher grade indigo crop was produced; annual production in South Carolina significantly increased from 110,000 to 1,122,000 pounds. Lindo was also apparently representing London merchants who were major importers. Trade flourished until the Revolutionary War, when trade with England all but stopped. But at that time cotton was coming into its own.

As an important aside, Moses Lindo was also one of three Jews (Israel Joseph and Michael Lazarus were the others) who donated money to Brown University in Providence, Rhode Island. Brown at that time did not accept Jews. After the donation, Lindo received the following letter from the university in 1770: "The sum of 20 pounds having been reported from Moses Lindo, a Jewish merchant of Charleston, it was thereupon voted that the children of Jews may be admitted to this institution, and entirely enjoy the freedom of their own religion without any restraint or imposition whatever."[15]

In 1773 a young, affluent Englishman came to South Carolina, leaving his wife and four children behind in England. Francis Salvador (who was born in England) was part of a wealthy, well known Jewish family of Portuguese and Dutch background. His family name was Jessuran Rodrigues, but at an earlier time the name Salvador (Savior) was chosen, probably to obscure their Jewish heritage at a critical time in Portugal. The changing of names was not unusual. His uncle and father-in-law, Joseph Salvador, was the first Jewish president of the Dutch East India Company, and later president of London's Bevis Marks Synagogue. He had significant financial resources, as he actually made substantial financial loans to the British government. There was even some thoughts in the London Jewish community of purchasing a part of South Carolina as a Jewish settlement, but that never developed.

Years before Francis Salvador came to South Carolina, Joseph Salvador had purchased some 100,000 acres in northwestern South Carolina, following a failed attempt by a London group to colonize and grow crops in an area called Ninety Six, near today's Greenwood. The purchased land was commonly called Jews' land. The area seemed to be a potentially great agricultural tract for lemon, oranges, lime, figs, pomengranates, sugar cane, olives and grape vines. Silk was tried but failed. Only indigo seemed to work out.

Joseph Salvador was a significant philanthropist for Jewish causes. He was also a member of the Bevis Marks' committee that aided some of the Jews who emigrated to Savannah in 1733.

Following the land purchase, his wealth, unfortunately, was dramatically impacted when the Dutch East India Company had serious financial difficulties, and a severe earthquake in Lisbon affected some of his investments. It was then that Francis Salvador, who was in South Carolina, bought 6,000 acres of his uncle's holdings in the Ninety-Six district, which had become the second largest community in the colony. Francis was hoping to revive Joseph's dwindling fortune.

Francis Salvador advertised for an overseer with knowledge of indigo, purchased 30 slaves, and became a farmer, planter and a frontiersman as required. Salvador became actively involved in the growing Revolutionary movement, and was elected to the First Provisional Congress from the Ninety Six district.

Ninety Six, now a very small town, was the most western English settlement in South Carolina, on the "Cherokee Path," and was so named because it was approximately 96 miles from the Cherokee trading center of Keowee, near present day Clemson. The "paths" were narrow, rough trails that adequately served pack horses, carts and early rural commerce. Many similar names were found along trading routes at that time, such as Twenty-five Mile Creek and Six Mile Mountain, both of which still exist.

Salvador served in the South Carolina Congress, representing his district in the first and second Provisional Congresses. He helped draft the state's constitution in 1776. His religion was of no apparent hindrance to his acceptance within the power structure of the state as he served on many committees, including chairman of Ways and Means, and a committee to establish credit to pay the militia. The Christological oath required to be sworn for membership in the provincial Congress was "...upon the Holy Evangelists of Almighty God" and to "... maintain and defend the Laws of God, the Protestant Religion and the Liberties of America." Apparently he took the required oath.

The 1776 constitution of South Carolina changed the former Provisional Congress into the General Assembly. Thus, Francis Salvador was the first Jew recorded to be holding legislative office in America.

Besides his legislative duties, Francis Salvador served in the militia defending against the British at the beginnings of the Revolutionary War. The Cherokee Indians, who were supporting the British (and were armed by them), were attacking frontier communities from time to time. During one attack, Salvador rode 28 miles to the home of a Major Williamson, to try to rally a defense against the Indians.

Salvador was a member of a small scouting party that was overwhelmed by the Indians, and he was scalped and died on August 1, 1776 at age 29. He is believed to be the first Jew to die in the Revolutionary War. A plaque to Salvador in Charleston reads:

Born an aristocrat, he became a democrat,
An Englishman, he cast his lot with America;
True to his ancient faith, he gave his life
For new hopes of human liberty and understanding.

Less than two years after Salvador's death, the South Carolina Assembly wrote a new constitution that would make it impossible for a known Jew to hold office. It made Protestantism the state religion and restricted anyone from being in the House, Senate or any high office unless he was Protestant. And only "churches" believing in the Christian religion could be incorporated. This would be in effect until 1790. The next South Carolina state constitution drafted after the Revolutionary War somewhat loosened the religious requirements, stating that, "no person was eligible to sit in the House of Representatives. . .unless he be of the Protestant religion. . .the established religion of the state. . ." although "all person who acknowledge one God, and future. . .rewards and punishments. . .and that God is publicly worshipped. . .shall be freely tolerated." One could say religion was on their minds, and Jews could be members, if they wanted to use the "freely tolerated" loophole.

The constitution written after the Revolutionary War removed these religious provisions. And with the British defeat Charles Town became Charleston.

Eight years after Francis Salvador's death, Joseph Salvador came to South Carolina at the age of 68. In England he tried to have naturalization laws changed to allow Jews to become citizens, but he was severely castigated for this and was once even jeered out of a theater. He never was able to become a citizen in England, so he chose to emigrate to the United States. He was never able to recover his financial losses in Europe.

He immediately settled in Ninety Six. While not much is known about his remaining years, he was able to sell many parcels of his acreage, enabling him to live fairly comfortably. A year after his arrival he moved to Charleston. The notice of his death on December 30, 1786 in the *Charleston Morning Post and Daily Advertiser* read in part:

> "He was formerly a most eminent merchant in England, being one of those who furnished that Government with a million of money in two hours notice, during the rebellion in the year 1745; and likewise was one of the greatest landholders in this country."

A codicil to Joseph Salvador's will left bequests to two congregations: a "German Jewish congregation," Beth Elohim, and a "Portuguese congregation," Beth Elohim

Unveh Shalom. This codicil provides some evidence that for a brief time there were two congregations in Charleston,[16] an extraordinarily rare occurrence for a city at that time. It was also apparent that it was the first time that Sephardim separated from an Ashkenazi congregation. (In Philadelphia in the 1795-1802 time period it was the other way around.) While the cause of the Charleston split is uncertain (possibly the Sephardic ritual was not followed), the two groups united no later than 1791. During the separation, however, the Sephardim would use their own cemetery.

In 1794 KKBE dedicated the first synagogue, costing about $20,000. The fact that some 40 years had elapsed between the establishment of Kahal Kadosh Beth Elohim and the laying of cornerstones for a synagogue was far from unusual at that time. There were an astonishingly small number of Jews and the primary concern was to create a viable economic base in the community. The prior synagogue was for a period of 12 years, in a renovated cotton gin factory on the same site.

The exterior of the new synagogue resembled a Georgian-style church, complete with a cupola, but was most clearly a Sephardic synagogue in the interior. Benches for the men were parallel to the north and south walls, and there was a Taba, an area for the hazzan to conduct the services and read the Torah. And, following Orthodox tradition, the women sat separately from the men in small balconies.

Eight cornerstones were laid, two by the most distinguished members, the others auctioned to the highest bidders. It would be the largest synagogue then in the United States. Dedicated on September 19, 1794 with an impressive procession of the Torahs into the sanctuary from the "old synagogue," on Hasell Street. Governor William Moultrie attended the dedication with state and municipal officials and clergy. The *South Carolina State-Gazette* wrote the next day:

> "Yesterday was consecrated to devine worship the Synagogue of the Jews, in Hazle-street (sic). The ceremony was attended by a numerous concourse of ladies and gentlemen; from which circumstances ...we can perceive those little prejudices and weaknesses that have for ages, disgraced the human character, to be wearing off and safely pronounce, that injured people, in the blessed climes of America, to have realized their promissed (sic) land. The shackles of religious distinction are no more; ...they are here admitted to the full priviledges of citizenship, and bid fair to flourish and be happy."

Charleston was then (as now) considered one of the most attractive cities in the growing country. It was also a center of theater and cultural life rivaling the cities in the northeast. In 1776 the Jewish population in Charleston was about 40 to 50 families, approximately 2% of the total population of 10,000. At that time Jews were less than .01% of the total population of the colonies.

Ira Rosenwaike, in a study of the Jewish population in 1820, printed by The American Historical Society, reported the following numbers: Charleston, 700; New York City, 550; Philadelphia, 450; Richmond, 200; Baltimore, 150; Savannah, 100, and 500 to 600 scattered elsewhere in the country. The total was 2,650 to 2,750 Jews out of a U.S. population of 9,638,000.[17]

From 1815 to 1840 there was over a five fold increase of U.S. Jews (from about 2,700 to 15,000), due to the initial influx of German Jews. The United States' general population in 1830 was approximately 12,866,000.

The massive immigration from Europe would start about 1860-1870. Few new Sephardic congregations were formed beyond this period. By mid-century there were some 110 synagogues in the U.S., mainly Ashkenazi.

7C

THE INITIAL REFORM MOVEMENT IN THE U. S.
The Reformed Society of Israelites

Whether it was a reflection of a growing change in the local population with greater Ashkenazi influence or the result of the Reform movement that had started in Europe in 1810 is uncertain, but by 1824 there was a desire in Kahal Kadosh Beth Elohim to present the Orthodox service in a way that would allow it to be more meaningful and understandable to many in the congregation. Some felt that the unvarying ritual, that was rapidly repeated almost by rote, was lacking in meaning for the American-born generation; some chose to find ways to alter their historic mode of religious practice.

The fact that most in the congregation had almost no Jewish education, and many of the congregants had the barest knowledge of Hebrew should not be surprising. Most congregations at that time did not devote much (if any) energy or resources to Hebrew education. The changes desired at KKBE seemed to be based, in part, on addressing religious and philosophical questions, such as whether both the oral law, and the rabbinical teachings are derived from God or whether there will be a Messiah. The desires also seemed equally focused on allowing the community to better understand Judaism and the prayer service. As noted earlier, when the translation of some prayers into English took place in New York in the 1760s, there were concerns of the consequences if English translations were actually used during services. These early Charlestonian reformers were apparently trying to make the service more accessible and meaningful to the community, and to stem a growing drift away from Judaism. As one person at the time stated, "not every one. . .has the means, and many have not the time, to acquire a knowledge of the Hebrew language" and English was "the language of the country."

There were forty seven signatures on a letter sent to the synagogue's board asking in a very dignified manner for: more decorum in the synagogue; shorter services; some prayers in English; elimination of repetitive prayers, and some sermons in English.[18] Some felt that a sermon in English would lend "some profit to their morals and even improve their mind." The synagogue sent no formal reply to the petition.

Such changes, which are considered mild today (but only to some), were considered momentous. In retrospect these initial changes to the Orthodox services would, in time, impact in one way or another the form of services of some 85% of American Jews. (The importance of the 1824-1843 time period in KKBE's searching for some degree of reform, deserves, I believe, a more detailed exposition.)

Change no matter how modest is still change. The Orthodox believed it would be a slippery slope, where modest changes would follow modest changes, until Orthodoxy itself would change.

Prayers were then entirely in Hebrew. Clearly the KKBE Sephardic leadership wanted no change, and there was absolutely no room for discussion or compromise. Changes were perceived as altering God's word and commandments.

Those desiring changes in the prayer services then left the congregation and moved their services to a social hall two blocks south of KKBE, to form The Reformed Society of Israelites. This was the first reform movement in the United States. The Society held services that contained some prayers in English, music and sermons or dissertations in English, and initiated mixed-gender seating. A handwritten prayer book containing prayers mostly in English and transliterated Hebrew was written by Isaac Harby, one of the driving forces with Abraham Moïse in the initial KKBE Reform movement. The original book is in private hands in Sumter, South Carolina.

Isaac Harby was a dynamic speaker, a journalist and a playwright. (One of his plays was performed in Charleston when President Madison visited.) Harby's family came to Charleston from Spain via Portugal, Morocco, London and Jamaica. In a speech by Harby, early in the Society's movement, he reiterated the desires of the reformers as noted earlier, but he also added some of the main ideas out of the recent Reform movement in Germany and northern France. This included non-belief in the coming of the Messiah, belief in the written law of the Torah as given to Moses on Mt. Sinai, but not necessarily belief in the oral law, which is the interpretation of the written law as defined by many rabbis over many centuries. Harby strongly felt that these subsequent rituals, interpretations and laws have resulted in an unclear, intricate, overly rule-oriented religious doctrine that made it difficult for the "average" Jew to follow, practice and believe in. He was president of Charleston's reform dissident group by 1827. By that time, however, much of the early enthusiasm generated from leaving KKBE by this lay movement was weakening. And they were about to lose two key members.

In a twist of fate Harby had to leave Charleston a few years later due to the death of his wife, Rachel, in 1827. Left alone with children, ages 4 to 15, he felt that the changed circumstances required him to follow a career in New York City. Hired as an editor for the *New York Mirror,* he moved in April 1828 and died in December of that same year.

David Carvalho, another leader of the Reform movement, left Charleston almost at the same time.

The Reform group had lost important, dynamic leaders, and in nine years from its initiation the group came back to KKBE. In addition to ongoing intense conflicts within families, there was continuing unrelenting social pressure from KKBE members against those wanting to change Judaism. Moreover, the reformers were unable to raise adequate funds for a synagogue. Whatever money they did raise was returned with interest.

While new to Charleston, sermons in English and prayers for the government in English had been previously used by Gershom Mendes Seixas in Shearith Israel in New York following the Revolutionary War. However, in New York's Shearith Israel no other significant changes would be made in the Orthodox service – and none were apparently desired at that time. KKBE however, was about to bring Reform Judaism to the United States. Most did not anticipate the years of difficulty, turmoil and conflict that lay ahead.

In 1836 two of The Reformed Society of Israelites desires were fulfilled – sermons in English and the method of payment for aliyahs (being called to the Torah) were changed. However, neither of these changes altered the Orthodox service. No prayers were omitted or changed in the sidur (prayer book), nor were any of the Hebrew prayers recited in English, nor was instrumental music used, nor were days of observance reduced. And a new constitution forbid members from adopting innovations that would "alter" the form of worship as practiced heretofore, or adopting changes in the Mosaic or Rabbinic Laws.

In the same year a new and major participant arrived on the scene. Gustavus Poznanski had been hired by KKBE to lead the congregation as "Reverend Hazzan."[19] Although not a rabbi, he was trained in Germany and had been in Shearith Israel in New York for two years. Poznanski was the community shochet (ritual slaughterer) and substitute hazzan. He was recommended by Issac

Leeser of Philadelphia, one of the strongest proponents of Orthodoxy. Leeser was editor of *The Occident,* an important Jewish periodical. He has been called the father of the Jewish press in America. He and Isaac M. Wise, a major proponent of Reform Judaism, would have intellectual battles in the pages of the publication. Poznanski also received a certificate of praise from Shearith Israel.

Clearly, neither Leeser nor Shearith Israel could have any idea that Poznanski would eventually be involved in bringing an Orthodox synagogue along the path to Reform. Poznanski, who was from Storchnest, Poland, had been hired in January 1837, and by May 1838 was designated hazzan for life! Poznanski had also spent time in Hamburg, viewing some of the reform ideas then bubbling in Germany.

While in Germany, he saw the painful and highly contentious transition of Orthodox synagogues to Reform. Poznanski would now find himself similarly leading KKBE through a series of conflicts.

Ironically, his work in bringing Reform Judaism to the U.S. would be done in a new synagogue building. A major fire would destroy the old synagogue and the Torahs in 1838.

Touro Synagogue and Cemetery, Newport, R.I.
Oldest synagogue in the United States (1763).

All photos © John T. Hopf

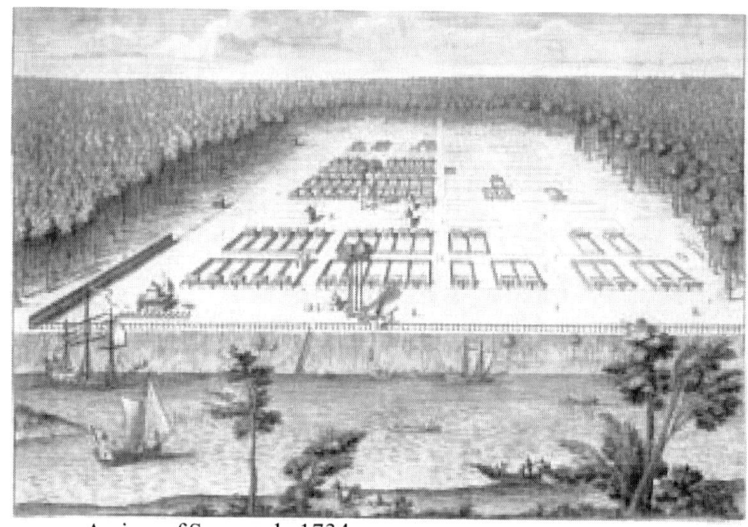

A view of Savannah, 1734.

Courtesy of the I.S. Phelps Stokes Collection, Miriam & Ira D. Wallach Div. of Arts, Prints and Photographs; New York Public Library; Astor, Lenox and Tilden Foundations.

Depiction of second synagogue building of Mickve Israel in Savannah, GA, consecrated in 1841, replacing the building of 1820.

Courtesy of Milton N. Kassel

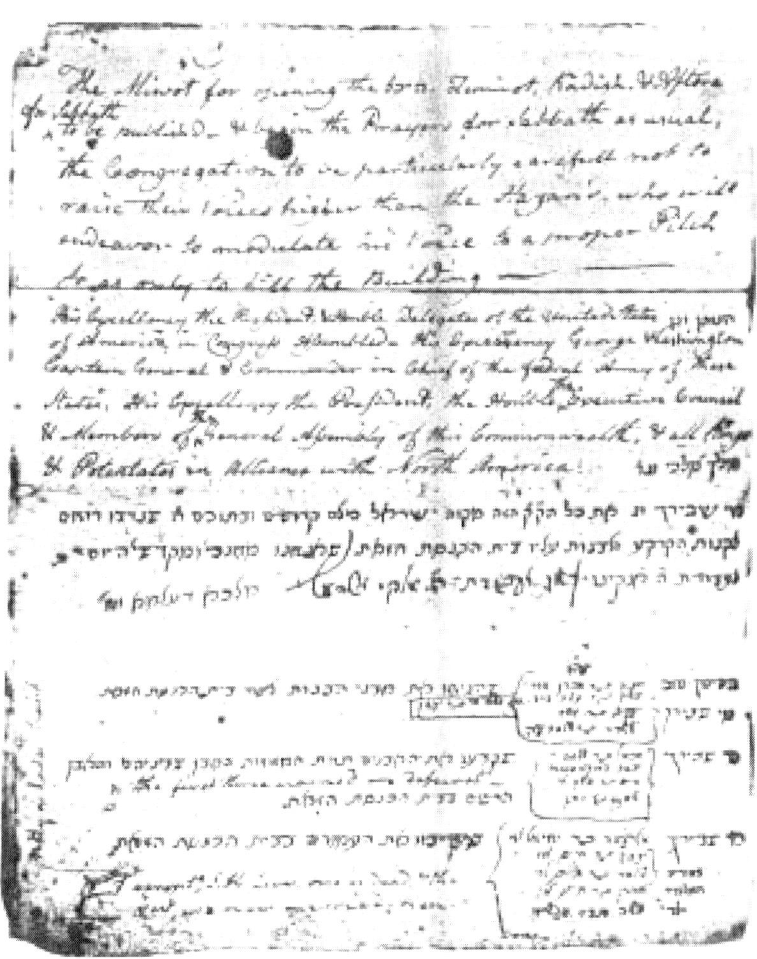

The Minot for opening the ... Tamid, Kadish & Aftera for Sabbath to be published — & begin the Prayers for Sabbath as usual, the Congregation to be particularly carefull not to raise their voices higher than the Hazan's, who will endeavor to modulate his voice to a proper Pitch so as only to fill the Building —

His Excellency the President & Hon'ble Delegates of the United States of America, in Congress Assembled — His Excellency George Washington Captain General & Commander in Chief of the federal Army of these States; His Excellency the President, the Hon'ble the Executive Council & Members of the General Assembly of this Commonwealth, & all Kings & Potentates in Alliance with North America.

Gershom Mendes Seixas notes for the dedication of Mikveh Israel Synagogue, Philadelphia, 1782.

Courtesy of American Jewish Historical Society, Newton, MA and New York, NY

Certificate of shipment of kosher beef from Philadelphia to Barbados, 1767.

Courtesy of the American Jewish Historical Society, Newton, MA and New York.

Charleston Harbor, prior to 1734.

Courtesy of the Emmet Collection, Miriam and Ira D. Wallach Div. of Arts, Prints and Photographs; New York Public Library, Astor, Lenox and Tilden Foundations.

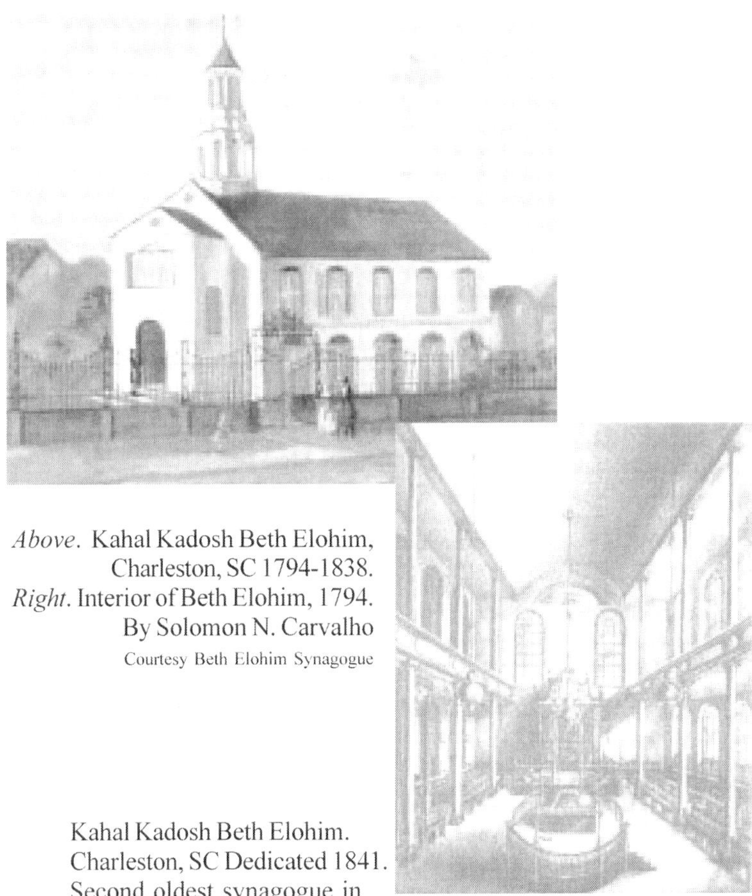

Above. Kahal Kadosh Beth Elohim, Charleston, SC 1794-1838.
Right. Interior of Beth Elohim, 1794.
By Solomon N. Carvalho
Courtesy Beth Elohim Synagogue

Kahal Kadosh Beth Elohim. Charleston, SC Dedicated 1841. Second oldest synagogue in the United States.
Courtesy of Jack Alterman.

7D

THE ESTABLISHMENT OF REFORM JUDAISM AT KKBE AND THE ORGAN CONTROVERSY 1840 - 1879

The original synagogue dedicated in 1794 was completely destroyed in 1838 by an extensive fire that ravaged the eastern part of the city, burning 145 acres eastward from King Street through the Ansonborough area. The local newspaper reported that one-third of the city was destroyed, including some 1,000 buildings demolished or damaged.

The current beautiful Greek Revival style synagogue was built by David Lopez, a member of KKBE, in 1840-1841. Greek Revival seems to have been the vogue in Charleston prior to the Civil War.

The Ark for the Torahs on the eastern wall of the synagogue is hand-carved of Santo Domingo mahogony, and it appears modeled after an Ark installed in the 1834 Crosby Street Synagogue of Shearith Israel in New York. Gustavus Pozanski, who served the New York synagogue may possibly have been a source of this design concept.

The new synagogue cost $40,000: $22,500 came from insurance; $8,250 from a state funded fire loan, and the balance from members and outside contributors.[20] The minutes of the congregation in 1838 stated that London, Curaço, Amsterdam and Barbados were unable to give financial assistance.

During the dedication in 1841 Poznanski noted,

> "...the plentitude of civil and religious privileges enjoyed by the House of Israel in this land of liberty and equal rights..."

And continued:

> "This synagogue is our temple, this city our Jerusalem, this happy land our Palestine, and as our fathers defended with their lives that temple, that city and that land, so will their sons defend this temple, this city, this land until the last drop of blood..."

It was ironic that just 21 years later the "defend... this city, this land" would strike home when his son later joined the Confederate Army and was killed at Secessionville. Gustavus Poznanski, Jr., who lived in New York with his family, traveled down to South Carolina to join and fight for the Confederacy, something he obviously did not have to do. It was another indication of the attachment felt by Jews toward Charleston and the South, a place that welcomed them.

Some members continued the drive towards modifying the services. As in Europe in the early 19th century the Orthodox viewed any change as portending further changes, as proved to be so both in the United States and abroad.

The vote by the membership in July 1840 for the use of an organ passed 46-40, with a stipulation that monies for the organ would be raised privately, outside of synagogue funds.

When the synagogue was completed in 1841, the organ was placed in the center of the small balcony, where, after a number of replacements it is still located. The minutes of the congregation indicated that an inscription should be placed over the organ in both Hebrew and English: *Praise him with Stringed Instruments and Organ*. Instrumental music was used in the Temples destroyed by Nebuchadnezzer in 586 BCE and the Romans in 70 CE.

But Orthodox, and most Conservative rabbis believe, that in commemoration of the tragedy of the destruction of the two ancient Temples, the joy of instrumental music should be banished from the synagogue, and this ban should remain until the time a new Temple is rebuilt in Jerusalem. An additional reason given is that the playing of instruments is considered to be improper work on the Sabbath.

The Orthodox members felt that an organ would bring on other reform changes – as it indeed had in Europe. Jacob Marcus states that the "...organ, a simple attractive musical instrument, was the Trojan horse that breached the Orthodox walls." After the vote on the organ, many (but not all) of the Orthodox members left, and proceeded to buy property on Wentworth Street, between Meeting Street and Anson Street, and formed Congregation Shearith Israel. They did not as yet build a synagogue. The two groups were now commonly known as the "Organ Congregation" and the "Remnants."

The presence and use of the organ (which was supported by Poznanski), led to harsh attempts by the Orthodox and the more conservative members to both weaken and embarass Poznanski and the Reform movement. Both his legitimacy and his Jewish parentage were questioned.[21] To resolve the matter, a request was sent to his former home in Poland, and the 1841 response stated that his mother was Jewish, a 'virtuous Jewish virgin' at the time of marriage, and that Gustavus was Jewish and legitimate. Things were really heating up, and this was even before the new synagogue was consecrated.

The synagogue was consecrated on March 19, 1841 with a grand procession. Poznanski made the well-known speech quoted earlier. There were many political moves that were underway regarding the future of Reform Judaism at KKBE. One external move was that KKBE chose not to participate in a proposed conclave of Jewish ministers in Philadelphia that year, that was organized by Isaac

Leeser to form a national organization of synagogues. KKBE felt that any central ecclesiastical authority would be dominated by Orthodox Germans, and the meeting was a gambit to weaken the Reform movement in favor of Orthodoxy.

A number of proposals by Poznanski that would change the services were turned down by the congregation. It appears that the congregation was then satisfied with the degree of Reform they had for the present. There were few who desired to further advance the limited changes that had taken place. Nor was there a major voice in KKBE addressing some of the philosphical and religious issues that would later define the Reform movement, except for some of the writing by Isaac Harby and others during the time of The Reformed Society of Israelites. But then again, very few were doing that in the United States at that time. KKBE was pushing Reform as fast as it could be accommodated by its members, and Poznaski was careful not to get too far ahead of congregational desires.

Poznanski felt opposition to reform came from those who personally disliked him, and from those who feared that further reform would evolve too far from Orthodox Judaism. A vote was taken in April 1843 whether KKBE should retain all Mosaic and Rabbinical laws. This was a major attempt to bring KKBE back to Orthodoxy. It failed by a very slim 27-24, and caused the Orthodox, and some wavering reformers, to feel that now was the time to recapture the synagogue for Orthodox Judaism.

On Passover 1843 Hazzan Poznanski added another very sensitive issue when he stated that in the future he would officiate only on one day for Pesach (Passover),and one day for Rosh Hashana (New Years) – (as it is written in the Torah). The Orthodox diaspora communities had celebrated two days for both Pesach and Rosh Hashana since the time of the Babylonian diaspora. Two days allowed Jews, in earlier times, to have some assurance that they were celebrating the holidays at the proper time, given the complexity of the Jewish lunar/solar calendar system. However, Poznanski noted that he had accurate calendars, and the second day was unnecessary. KKBE's board believed that Poznanski's position on observing the holidays was "a violation of the Constitution, and would create discord and anarchy." This desire to eliminate the second day (which eventually failed) resulted in a major move by the Orthodox community to regain KKBE. People from Charleston's Shearith Israel and the Orthodox remaining within KKBE, proposed to eliminate any and all changes that had been made in the services, throw out the organ, erect a mikvah and fire Poznanski.

On April 30, 1843, a group supporting the return to Orthodoxy called a meeting with the stated purpose "to stop the progress of Reform in our Synagogue, and to prevent the destruction of our holy religion." Poznanski was also charged with dividing the "once happy congregation," and introducing German doctrines that would only "produce a generation of deists." When he was asked where these changes to the religion would end, he replied, ". . that he knew no stopping place to Reform in this enlightened age."

Then in an unusual move, ten people from Shearith Israel were made voting members of KKBE (in what later proved to be an illegal process). This tactic tipped the voting majority in favor of Orthodoxy, and the traditionalists didn't lose any time in changing the services as they wished: banning instrumental music; ordering Poznanski to return his books and synagogue possessions, and taking control of the synagogue. In a last ditch effort the organist tried to play music at the services. Poznanski later stated he feared a "disgraceful conflict and perhaps bloodshed."[22] Legal action was then undertaken to determine if the synagogue was illegally taken over by the supporters of Orthodoxy.

THE COURT CASE: REFORM OR ORTHODOX?

In October 1843 the reformers filed charges in the Court of Common Pleas in Charleston. The case was taken up in the Spring Term, 1844. It was called "In the case of the State ex relatione A. Ottolengui v. G. V. Anker and others." The case was to adjudicate whether the decision to admit the people from Shearith Israel was illegal, and whether the decision to allow them to vote on synagogue issues was legal and in accordance with the synagogue's charter. The reformers believed that the people were added to KKBE membership illegally, and: ". . .had intruded themselves into the enjoyment of the liberties, privileges and franchise of members of a body corporate called the Charleston Jewish Congregation of Beth Elohim or House of God. . ." They felt that the "intruders" had exercised the privileges of membership, and thus the vote changing KKBE from a Reform synagogue to an Orthodox one was illegal.

The unusual move to resolve the issue through the civil court system was based on the belief that the votes effecting changes in the congregation violated the charter. They felt that they were not attempting to get a civil court decision on a religious conflict issue; but that's what the court case would essentially do.

A jury trial took place in April 1844 over a four-day period. The decision was that the admission of the "new members" was illegal, and thus the ensuing votes changing the synagogue from Reform to Orthodox Judaism was illegal. In January 1845 the Orthodox appealed the decision to the South Carolina Court of Errors and Appeals, stating they had actually never left KKBE, were always members and had the right to vote. In January 1846 the appeals court concurred with the decision of the lower court, and refused to set aside the judgment.

The decision of the appeals court stated that:

1) the supposed new members had paid no dues to the synagogue in the interim;

2) they had taken no part in meetings of the synagogue;

3) they formed another congregation;

4) attended another congregation in violation of the constitutional rules, and

5) they had applied for readmission – which isn't done if you are already a member.

It was over for the moment. It is interesting to note that during these dragged out court proceedings (2 years and 3 month, including appeal), the Reform and Orthodox groups shared a shochet (ritual slaughterer) and alternated on a weekly basis in the use of the KKBE synagogue (the only one in town). Such a commendable solution probably could not be used today.

Those who wanted to retain Orthodoxy then built a synagogue called Shearith Israel in 1847, with 52 families as members initially. The synagogue on the north side of Wentworth Street, between Meeting and Anson Streets, remained there until the Civil War, when it was damaged by shelling and could not be used. It was later sold to the Roman Catholic Church and used for black worshippers.

While this battle between Reform and Orthodoxy was playing out, the reform movement had already started its rapid spread northwards. Reform Judaism was being established at several synagogues – Har Sinai in Baltimore in 1842 (with mainly German immigrants adopting the Hamburg Temple prayer book), and Temple Emanu-El in New York, 1845. The latter congregation had written to Poznanski seeking "such instruction and information" to allow them to conduct "in a congregation to be formed from our society, such a service, as freed from abuses tolerated hitherto, shall arouse and quicken devotion, and thus uplift the heart of God." Then, Reform Judaism reached Albany, New York in 1846 with Isaac M. Wise, who proved to be an important and dynamic figure in its further development.

ISAAC M. WISE – ALMOST AT KKBE

In 1847 Hazzan Poznanski resigned from KKBE (for the final time). He had been at KKBE for eleven turbulent years that included the fire; the rebuilding of the synagogue; a resignation and return; the organ controversy and court case, and the internal struggles between the Reform and Orthodox members. KKBE looked for someone to carry forward the Reform movement. They selected Dr. Julius Landsburger of Breslow, Prussia. After an extended period of negotiations (where he asked about local climate and sanitary conditions), the congregation selected him, and then learned that he had taken another position in Europe.

During the ensuing search for a rabbi, KKBE chose to bring Isaac M. Wise of Albany, New York to Charleston for an interview and a brief trial in 1850.

On coming to Charleston there was an immediate conflict of culture and personalities between Poznanski and Wise. (Poznanski was one of five people on the search committee looking for the new rabbi.) Wise stated later that from the first ride into Charleston from the dock, he saw Poznanski as pompous and arrogant, particularly when Poznaski tried to coach Wise on proper manners in meeting other people, and tried to correct, what Poznanski felt, were "Germanisms." Wise in turn responded, "If there are, you would substitute Polisms (Polanisms) for them."[23]

There was an incident during Wise's visit to Charleston that should be mentioned. During a debate involving Wise, Dr. Morris Raphall (an Orthodox leader who happened to be in Charleston) asked Wise whether he believed in a Messiah, or in bodily resurrection. Wise responded with a loud "No" to both. Wise's statements regarding Reform Judaism put him in conflict with many members of his first congregation in Albany.

At another talk during his Charleston visit, Raphall decried the new Reform movement. He felt that the freedom Jews were experiencing in America was weakening the bonds of rabbinical authority and control, and this was leading to "folly" by a handful of Jews.

Born in Bohemia and coming to the United States in 1846, Wise found a pulpit in Albany, New York. He used the titles of rabbi and Doctor of Divinity, neither of which were true. Some thirty years later a Rabbi Jastrow said about rabbinical titles: "Here a man qualifies himself, ordaining himself; he is his own college, his own professor, his own diploma. He is what he claims to be."

Wise's attempts to bring reform measures to his traditional Albany synagogue led to increasing internal dissent with most of his membership. The positions he took in Charleston, regarding his non-belief in the Messiah and in bodily resurrection, rapidly found its way to Albany and led him into additional major conflicts with his membership. On his return to Albany from the Charleston "debate" with Raphall, a fist fight broke out during a New Year's service between his supporters and the majority of traditionalists. The police were actually called to quell the incident.

Following this very lively period of the clashing of ideas in Charleston, Isaac Wise was offered the position of rabbi at KKBE, and he accepted. But later he reconsidered this move, possibly it is thought, due to his wife's concerns about the high humidity and occurrences of yellow fever. But it is possible that the main reason Wise did not accept the position was due to Poznanski's presence. He might have seen Poznaski waiting in the wings, as the former local chacham, ready to interfere and activate, when he felt appropriate, his own clique of supporters. Wise's own thoughts are not known. In his *Reminiscences* he wrote that KKBE was composed of "American aristocrats. . .of Portuguese descent."[24]

As this was the second turn-down in a short time, the board was quite perturbed and sent a bill to Wise for $149.31 to cover the cost of the round-trip. There is no record of a check being received. Clearly the check is not in the mail.

Wise and his supporters organized Anshe Emeth in Albany, NY in 1850, where he first instituted mixed-gender seating and a choir. He left that synagogue in 1854 to be leader of Bene Yeshurn in Cincinnati, and became a powerful and articulate advocate, writer, educator and organizer in developing the intellectural base for the Reform movement. In the same year he also founded *The Israelite*, which he edited and published for some 50 years.

Wise helped establish the Union of American Hebrew Congregations in 1873 and the Hebrew Union College in 1875. Others important in the movement at that time included David Einhorn of Har Sinai in Baltimore, Max Lilienthal of Bene Israel in Cincinnati, and Bernard Felsenthal of Sinai Congregation in Chicago.

Poznanski continued his attempt to be the power behind the throne. Rabbi Julius Eckman was selected and became KKBE's first ordained rabbi. Eckman denounced Poznanki as "not only an infidel, but inimically opposed to the very institution of Judaism." Poznanski tried to dictate to Eckman from the beginning. A struggle within the synagogue broke out with Shearith Israel supporters involved. According to Rabbi Leeser of Philadelphia, Eckman was making "many and blessed exertions to restore religion to its Orthodox standards among his flock." The Reform members stated what is obvious, that if they knew the reform measures taken over the previous ten years would be in jeopardy, Eckman would not have been hired. The battle continued, and Eckman resigned serving only one year. The congregation saw that any desired changes had to be defended and protected or else they would, in time, disappear.

Possibly further fueling the crucial division between

the Reform KKBE and the Orthodox in Shearith Israel, was the ongoing resentment that the Orthodox had been deprived of their beautiful, and some believed, rightful synagogue.

KKBE'S ROLE IN REFORM JUDAISM: A RETROSPECTIVE

What then was the role of KKBE in the Reform movement up to this point? Was it just to bring music into the services and celebrating Rosh Hashana on one day instead of two? KKBE's role turned out to be the initiator of Reform Judaism in the United States. They were the first to undertake the attempt to modify the Orthodox ritual in this country. Some might say, in hindsight, that the changes of 1824 and the 1840s were relatively minor, and that they never confronted or addressed the religious doctrinal issues in depth that later would be at the crux of early Classical Reform Judaism. There could be a number of reasons for not addressing doctrinal issues:

1. These were the first people in the United States to confront the monumental task of proposing to alter Orthodoxy, where even the most "minor" change was seen as undermining Judaism. The first small steps were huge hurdles at that time. Maybe the congregation understood what might be attainable, and limited their goals. As well, they had to defend any inroads that they had made (as they quickly learned), in retaining whatever degree of Reform Judaism they had evolved.

2. Few members actually wanted to go to the ramparts. They were mainly, but not completely, satisfied with the services, and tended to be socially and religiously conservative. They were not interested in completely revamping the religion, even if they actually understood all the larger implications. The broader and more deeply intellectual issues that were brought up by Harby, Wise, Raphall and others (concerning belief in the Messiah, resurrection,

and whether both the Mosaic and Rabbinic Laws were God-given), were not issues that confronted the average congregant's daily lives. There seemed to be no one with the intellectual depth, and burning fervor at that time in KKBE to confront these issues in a national arena. They did not have sufficient Hebraic education to handle the more philosophical and religious doctrine issues.

Gustavus Poznanski brought ideas for changes in the services that were certainly ahead of his time, but he did not publish much about his purposes or the philosophy of the new Reform Judaism in letters or publications. He became more reform-minded during his time in Charleston. Whether he himself, internally, had a mission to bring Reform Judaism to KKBE starting in 1840, or found himself driven by the congregation and went along, is open for debate. He never addressed the over-arching basis for the directions taken. When there was heavy opposition, he tended to withdraw for another day. However, what was done, was to alter the services and make them more welcoming and understandable to those in the community that wanted these changes.

While KKBE was the first congregation to grapple with establishing Reform Judaism in what was an Orthodox congregation, Har Sinai Verein in Baltimore was the first to organize itself as a Reform congregation from its inception in 1842.

What KKBE accomplished was actually larger than the changes themselves. It was setting an environment for further changes. They laid the platform for others who brought along further and more substantial changes, at a time when the community was ready to address the doctrinal issues altering Jewish services. KKBE courageously took the first steps in the United States.

Yet, KKBE was not a major player in the future intellectual blooming and broad establishment of Reform Judaism. The synagogue had continuing difficulties – there was no uniform direction on liturgy or Reform philosophy at that time. KKBE retained what they had accomplished. They did not press forward in developing Reform Judaism. But many other synagogues were also quite hesitant in taking the "next step" at that time, such as the removal of kippahs (head coverings) and the dispensation of tallesim (prayer shawls).

When Poznanski retired, he remained in Charleston for a while, then went to New York and requested seats at Shearith Israel. Annoyed with what he had done in Charleston, the congregation was, at first, unwilling, but later relented and alloted five seats to the family.[25]

In 1862 he was killed by a horse carriage on the streets of New York.

7E

THE IMPACT OF THE CIVIL WAR ON CHARLESTON'S SYNAGOGUES

The next great issue for Charleston, and the nation, was the Civil War. In 1864, when Gen. William Tecumseh Sherman was in Savannah, it was commonly believed that he would march up the coast and ravage Charleston. Valuables from private homes, as well as from places of worship, were sent to Columbia, South Carolina, its capital, for safekeeping. KKBE sent its Torahs, the organ, the Torah remonim (silver ornamentation) and the chandeliers, and St. Michael's Church sent its bells. Sherman, however, calling Charleston "a mere desolated wreck," and noting that the Union shelling had already destroyed the city, took his Army to Columbia. He wrote, "I look at Columbia as quite as bad as Charleston and I doubt if we shall spare the public buildings. . ."

As you may know Sherman went to Columbia, and those items transported for safekeeping were destroyed. (St. Michaels' bells, which are the ones in current use, were seriously damaged and were sent back to England for recasting.) Sometimes planning ahead is a good idea, but sometimes it just doesn't seem to work.

A year after the surrender at Appomattox, KKBE was still in a dilapidated state and Rabbi Leeser of Philadelphia, who was in Charleston in 1866, noted that there was "dust resting on the furniture and benches, many panes of glass broken, (and) the ceiling crushed in many places by the explosion of shells that penetrated the roof." The synagogue had been closed for periods during the war. Leeser also found Shearith Israel on Wentworth Street "so greatly injured. . .as to almost render it useless as a place of worship."[26]

There was later consideration of moving KKBE from Hasell Street, due to the damage and the congestion on the street, but wiser heads prevailed, and this was rejected. The congregation, the Jews and the general population were now just trying to survive after the Civil War. Poverty and desolation were everywhere. KKBE lost one-third of its membership due to the war's death toll and because many members were impoverished. There was a general weakening and dispersion of the community.

The members of Shearith Israel tried to gain control over the synagogue building, but KKBE members appealed to the U.S. Army (then managing the city); the building remained the property of KKBE. The two synagogues then combined briefly after the trauma of the war, each compromising in regard to services. The economy of the entire area was in a most serious and long term economic depression. The area had lost its agricultural base, and the south had never diversified into manufacturing. It took a long time indeed for the area to heal its economic and social wounds.

At this point, the great migration of Jews through Castle Garden and Ellis Island increased from a trickle to a flood. In 1880 the Western Hemisphere had 3.5% of the world's Jewish population. By 1933 it was 30%. I would like to quote what one immigrant saw as he came into New York harbor in 1882. Abraham Cahan, the former editor of the Yiddish *Forward* newspaper, wrote: "The magnificent verdure of Staten Island, the tender blue of sea and sky, the dignified bustle of passing craft – above all, those floating, squatting, multitudinously-windowed palaces which I consequently learned to call ferries. It was all so utterly unlike anything I had ever seen or dreamed of before. It unfolded itself like a divine revelation."[27]

This long journey starting in the Iberian Peninsula some 500 years ago is over. But the courage and the tenacity of these pioneering Sephardi and Ashkenazi people produced a heritage and a presence that remains a part of all the old synagogues and communities where the first Jews came to the New World.

SOURCE CITATIONS

CHAPTER 1

1. Carr, 84-85
2. Johnson, 176-177
3. Shannon, 60 & 75
4. Gerber, 113
5. Kamen (Spanish Inquisition), 29
6. Gerber, 117
7. Keller, 255
8. Roth (A History of the Jews), 225
9. Lagassé, 2863
10. Kamen, (Spanish Inquisition), 57-58
11. Fletcher, 167
12. Peters, 99
13. Kamen, (Spanish Inquisition), 189
14. Kamen, (Empire), 344

CHAPTER 2

1. Gerber, 286
2. Kamen, (Empire.) , 22
3. Roth, (A History of the Jews) , 250
4. Keller, 262-263
5. Ibid. 263-264
6. Kantor, 183
7. Faber, 6-7
8. Williams, 98-99

CHAPTER 3

1. Keller, 310-311
2. Cohen-Sherbock, 589
3. Fuson, 51-52
4. Freyre, 36
5. First Rabbi in the New World,
   Chapters in American Jewish History, Chapter 82
   American Jewish Historical Soc. May 4, 2001
6. Russel-Wood, 108-109
7. Lebeson, 47
8. Marcus, (Early American Jewry, Vol.1) p.16

CHAPTER 4

1. Keller, 312
2. Rochlin, 1-3 & 6-7
3. Congregation Mickve Israel-Emanuel 'Synagogue Guidebook',
   3rd Ed., Curaçao, 21-22
4. Faber, 22-23

5. Arbell, 183-184 citing from 'The Parliamentary History of England from the Earliest Period to the Year 1803, London 1814, v. 33 1781-1783, 225
6. Keller, 312
7. Ibid, 316; Lockhart, 23
8. H.M. Public Record Office, Calendar of State Papers (Colonies), No. 234, 294, cited by Arbell, 203
9. Arbell, 204
10. Lebeson, 52-54

CHAPTER 5

1. Wright, 83
2. Marcus, (Colonial American Jew, Vol.1) , 414
3. Lebeson, 83
4. Marcus, (Early American Jewry, Vol. 2), 518-519
5. Jewish Rights In Early Connecticut
   Chapters in American Jewish History, Chapter 80
   American Jewish Historical Society, Aug. 14, 1998
6. A Case of Blasphemy
   Chapters in American Jewish History, Chapter 99
   American Jewish Historical Society, Jan. 15, 1999
7. Fein, 31-34; Schappes, 168
8. Marcus, (Colonial American Jew, Vol.1), 456
9. Hagy, 35-37
10. Marcus (American Jewry Documents, Eighteenth Century) 296-302
11. Swift, 13

CHAPTER 6

1. Milton, 116 and 156
2. Marcus, (Jew in the American World), 28-30
3. Translation from the New York Public Library Picture Collection. A copy of original letter is in the archives of the Museum of the City of New York
4. Taylor, 256
5. Lebeson, 59-60 and Rink, 233-234
6. Marcus, (Early American Jewry, Vol.1), 22
7. Marcus, (Early Jewry, Vol.1) , 30
8. Keller, 317; Schappes, 4-6
9. Lebeson, 59
10. Pool, 31-32
11. Labeson, 60-1
12. Marcus, (Early American Jewry, Vol. 1), 32
13. Pool, 33
14. Marcus (Early America Jewry, Vol. 1), 55-56
15. Pool, 44
16. Lebeson, 80
17. Proceedings of the American Jewish Historical Society ,

Lyons Collection, No. 172, Vol. XXXVII (1920), 10-11, 17-18
18. Faber, 114
19. Touro Synagogue Brochure
National Park Service U.S. Dept. of Interior, 1983
20. Marcus, (Colonial American Jew) Vol. 1), 314-315
21. Marcus, (Early Jewry, Vol.1) , 154-155
22. Brands, 110, 326
23. Schappes, 79-81
24. Pool, 421-422, 425-426
25. Francis Salvador and American Independence Chapters in American Jewish History
American Jewish Historical Society, June 30, 2000
(Article has error in relationship of Francis Salvador to Joseph Salvador. Francis is his nephew and son-in-law.)
26. Marcus, (Colonial American Jew, Vol.1), 356-357
27. Capps, 45; Coleman, 22
28. Levy and Belzer
A History of Congregation Mickve Israel
Congregation Mikve Israel, Savannah, GA
29. Marcus, (Colonial, Vol.1), 360-361
30. Simonhoff, 13
31. Faber, 111-113
32. "The Organs of Congregation Mickve Israel". Short unpublished paper from Mickve Israel. Condensed from "Organs of Savannah" by William P. Clarke Jr., Pub. 2001
33. Wolf, 32
34. Marcus, (Early Jewry, Vol. 2) , 55-57
35. Denton, 106
36. Marcus, (Early Jewry, Vol. 2) , 130-134
37. Faber, 109
38. Wolf, 143-145

CHAPTER 7

1. Osborne, 18
2. Jones, 27
3. Craven, 98-99
4. Shaftesbury Papers, 217-218
5. Weir, 59
6. Shaftesbury Papers, 162
7. Lebeson, 74
8. Shaftesbury Papers, 113
9. Ibid, 311-312
10. Ibid, 99
11. Hagy, 6
12. Ravenel, 48
13. Fraser, 22, 27
14. Marcus, (Colonial American Jew, Vol. 1) , 345
15. Lebeson, 83-84

16. Breibart, (Two Congregations), 360-363; Hagy, 64-68; Marcus (United States Jewry, Vol. 1), 221
17. Rosenswaike, American Jewish Historical Quarterly Vol. LIII, No.2, Dec. 1963, 152
18. The Americanization of the Reform Movement Chapters in American Jewish History, Chapter 58 American Jewish Historical Society, Feb. 27, 1998
19. Simonhoff, 276-277
20. Breibart (The Synagogues of KKBE), 12
21. Hagy, 247-248
22. Ibid. 252
23. Ibid. 264-265
24. Wise, Isaac M. (Reminiscences)
25. Pool, 430
26. Reznikoff, 162
27. Sachar, (The Course of Modern Jewish History) , 311

BIBLIOGRAPHY

Adams, James Truslow. *Provincial Society*
Quadrangle Books, 1955

Arbell, Mordechai. *The Jewish Nation of the Caribbean*
Jerusalem, Israel: Gefen Publishing House, 2002

Ausubel, Nathan. *Pictorial History of the Jewish People*
New York: Crown Publishing, NY, 1984 (First Revised Edition)

Barnavi, Eli. (ed.) *A Historical Atlas of the Jewish People*
New York: Schocken Books, 1992

Barnett, R. and Abraham Levy. *The Bevis Marks Synagogue*
Oxford: University Press, 1970 (Pamphlet)

Barzun, Jacques. *From Dawn to Decadence*
New York: Harper Collins, 2000

Bloom, Herbert. *The Economic Activities of the Jews in Amsterdam in the 17th and 18th Centuries,* Williamsport: 1937

Bowes, Frederick P. *The Culture of Early Charleston*
Chapel Hill, NC: The University of North Carolina Press, 1942

Boxer, C.R. *The Dutch Seaborne Empire, 1600-1800*
New York: Penguin Books, 1965

Brands, H. W. *The First American*
New York: Doubleday, 2000

Breibart, Solomon. *The Synagogues of Kahal Kadosh Beth Elohim,* Charleston, SC: Sisterhood of Kahal Kadosh Beth Elohim, 1999

Breibart, Solomon. *Two Jewish Congregations in Charleston, SC Before 1791: A New Conclusion,*
American Jewish History, 69, Vol. LXIX No. 3, March 1980

Brown, Ira L. *The Georgia Colony*
New York: Macmillian Co., 1970

Butler, Jon. *Awash in a Sea of Faith*
Boston: Harvard University Press, 1990

Butler, Jon. *Becoming America*
Boston: Harvard University Press, 2000

Campbell, P.F. *An Outline of Barbados History*
Bridgetown: 1973

Capps, Clifford S., and Eugene Burney. *Georgia*
Thomas Nelson Inc., 1972

Carr, Raymond. (ed.) *Spain- A History*
Oxford: Oxford University Press, 2000

Chayet, Stanley. *American Jewish Archievers*
April 1964 Vol. XVI No. 1

Cohn-Sherbok, Dan. *Blackwell Dictionary of Judaica*
Oxford: Blackwell Publishers, 1992

Coleman, Kenneth, ed. *A History of Georgia*
University of Georgia Press, 1977

Craven, Wesley Frank. *The Colonies in Transition, 1660-1713*
New York: Harper Row, 1968

Dawidowicz, Lucy S. *What is the Use of Jewish History?*
New York: Schocken Books, NY, 1992

Deaton, Stanley K. *Revolutionary Charleston, 1765-1800*
Gainsville: University of Florida, 1997

DeJong, Gerald F. *The Dutch in America, 1609-1974*
Boston: Twayne Publishers, 1975

DeSola Pool, David and Tamara. *An Old Faith in the New World,* New York: Columbia University Press, 1955

Dilard, Maud Esther. *An Album of New Netherland*
New York: Twayne Publishers, 1963

Dimont, Max I. *Jews, God and History*
Signet, New York: New American Library, 1962

Dimont, Max I. *The Jews of America*
New York: Simon & Schuster, 1978

Elliott, J.H. *Imperial Spain, 1469-1716*
New York: Penguin Books, 1970

Elzas, Barnett A. *The Jews of South Carolina*
Spartenburg, SC: The Reprint Co., Spartanburg, 1983

Ezratty, Harry A. *500 Years in the Jewish Caribbean*
Baltimore: Omni Arts Inc., 1997

Faber, Eli. *The Jewish People in America; A Time For Planting*
Baltimore: Johns Hopkins Press, 1992

Fein, Isaac M. *The Making of An American Jewish Community*
Philadelphia: The Jewish Publication Society, 1971

Friedman, Murray, Ed. *Jewish Life in Philadelphia, 1830-1940*
Philadelphia: Ishi Publications, 1983

Fletcher, Richard. *Moorish Spain*
New York: Henry Holy and Co., 1992

Fortune, Stephen Alexander. *Merchants and Jews, the Struggle for British West Indian Commerce 1650-1750*
Gainesville, 1984

Fraser, Jr., Walter J. *Charleston!, Charleston!*
Columbia, SC: University of South Carolina Press, 1989

Freund, Miriam K. *Jewish Merchants in Colonial America*
New York: Berman's Jewish Book House, 1939

Freyre, Gilberto *The Masters and the Slaves*
New York: Alfred Knopf, 1971

Fuson, Robert H. *The Log of Christopher Columbus*
Camden, ME: International Marine Publishing Co., 1987

Gerber, Jane S. *The Jews of Spain*
New York: The Free Press, 1992

Goodman, Abram Vossen. *American Overture*
Philadelphia: Jewish Publication Society, 1947

Glassman, Ronald M. *Political History of Latin America*
New York: Funk & Wagnalls, 1969

Gullan-Whur, Margaret. *Within Reason, A Life of Spinoza*
New York: St. Martin's Press, 2000

Hagy, James William. *This Happy Land*
University of Alabama Press, 1993

Haliczer, Stephen. *Inquisition and Society in the Kingdom of Valencia* Berkley, CA: University of California Press, 1990

Hallendorff, Carl. *History of Sweden*
New York: AMS Press, 1970

Hertzberg, Arthur. *The Jews in America*
New York: Simon and Schuster, 1989

Jameson, J. Franklin. (ed.) *Narratives of New Netherland, 1609-1664,* New York: Charles Scribner's Sons, 1909

Jick, Leon A. *The Americanization of the Synagogue, 1820-1870,* Brandeis University Press, 1976

Johnson, Paul. *A History of the Jews*
New York: Harper Perennial, 1987

Jones, Lewis P. *South Carolina*
Columbia, SC: Sandlapper Press, 1971

Jones, Virgil Carrington. *The Civil War at Sea*
New York: Holt, Rinehart, Winston, 1962

Kamen, Henry. *Empire*
New York: Harper Collins Publishers, 2003

Kamen, Henry. *Phillip of Spain*
New Haven: Yale University Press, 1997

Kamen, Henry. *The Spanish Inquisition*
New Haven: Yale University Press, 1997

Kantor, Mattis. *The Jewish Timeline Encyclopedia*
Jason Aronson Inc., 1992

Karp, Abraham J. (ed.) *The Jewish Experience in America*
Waltham, MA: American Jewish Historical Society, 1969

Kedourie, Elie (ed.) *Spain and the Jews*
London: Thames and Hudson, Ltd., 1992

Keller, Werner. *Diaspora*
New York: Harcourt, Brace and World Inc., 1966

Lagassé, Paul. (ed.) *The Columbia Encyclopedia*
New York: Columbia University Press, 2000

Learsi, Rufus. *The Jews in America – A History*
Cleveland and New York: World Publishing Co., 1954

Lebeson, Anita Libman. *Pilgrim People*
New York: Minerva Press, 1975

Lewis, Theodore, *History of Touro Synagogue*
Bulletin of the Newport Historical Society
Number 159, Vol. 48, Part 3, 1975

Lockhart, James. *Early Latin America*
Cambridge: Cambridge University Press, 1983

Madariaga, Salvador de. *Christopher Columbus*
New York: Unger, 1967

Marcus, Jacob R. *American Jewry – Documents Eighteenth Century*
Cincinnatti: Hebrew Union College Press, 1959

Marcus, Jacob R. *The Colonial American Jew, 1492-1776*
(3 Vols.) Detroit: Wayne State University Press, 1970

Marcus, Jacob R. (ed.), *The Jew in the American World*
Detroit: Wayne State University Press, 1996

Marcus, Jacob R. *Early American Jewry* (2 Vols.)
The Jewish Publication Society, 1951

Marcus, Jacob R. *Memoirs of American Jews, 1775-1865*
(3 Vols.) Philadelphia: The Jewish Publication Society, 1955

Marcus, Jacob R. *Studies in American Jewish History*
Cincinnati: Hebrew Union College Press, 1969

Marcus, Jacob R. *United States Jewry, 1776-1985* (Vol. 1)
Detroit: Wayne State University Press, 1989

Milton, Giles. *Big Chief Elizabeth*
New York: Farrer, Straus & Giroux, 2000

McFarlane, Anthony *The British In the Americas, 1480-1815*
Harlow, England: Longman Group Ltd., 1994

Myers, Gustavus. *History of Bigotry in the United States*
New York: Random House, 1943

Osborne, Anne Riggs. *The South Carolina Story*
Columbia, SC: Sandlapper Publishing Inc., 1988

Perry, Mary Elizabeth. *Cultural Encounters*
Berkley, CA: University of California Press, 1991

Pestana, Carla Gardina. *Inequality in Early America*
Hanover and London: University Press of New England, 1999

Peters, Edward. *Inquisition*, New York: The Free Press, 1988
Philipson, David. *Reform Movement in Judaism*
New York: Macmillan Co., 1931

Poston, Jonathan H. *The Buildings of Charleston*
Columbia, SC: University of South Carolina Press, 1997

Ravenel, Harriott Horry. *Charleston*
New York: Macmillan, 1931

Reznikoff, Charles. *The Jews of Charleston*
Philadelphia: The Jewish Publication Society, 1950

Ridley, Jasper. *Bloody Mary's Martyrs*
New York: Carrol & Graf Publishers, 2001

Ridley, Jasper. *Henry VIII*
New York: Viking Penguin, 1985

Rink, Oliver A. *Holland on the Hudson*
Ithaca, NY: Cornell University Press, 1986

Rochlin, Harriet. *Pioneer Jews*, Los Angeles: Knapp Press, 1984

Rosen, Robert N. *Confederate Charleston*
Columbia, SC: University of South Carolina Press, 1994

Rosen, Robert N. *The Jewish Confederates*
Columbia, SC: University of South Carolina Press, 2000

Rosenwaike, Ira. *The Jewish Population of the United States as Estimated from the Census of 1820*
American Jewish Historical Quarterly, 53 (Dec. 1963); 153-57

Roth, Cecil. *A History of the Jews*
New York: Schocken Books, 1961

Roth, Cecil. *A History of the Marranos*
New York: Sepher-Hermon Press, 1992

Rubin, Saul Jacob. *Third To None*
Savannah: Congregation Mickve Israel, 1983

Russel-Wood, A.J.R. *The Portuguese Empire 1415-1808*
Baltimore: The Johns Hopkins University Press, 1992

Rye, Scott. *Men and Ships of the Civil War*
Longmeadow Press, 1995

Sacher, Abram Leon. *A History of the Jews*
New York: Knopf, 1974

Sachar, Howard M. *The Course of Modern Jewish History*
Cleveland and New York: The World Publishing Co., 1958

Sarna, Jonathan D. *The American Jewish Experience*
New York and London: Holmes & Meier, 1986

Schappes, Morris D., Ed. *A Documentary History of the Jews in the United States, 1654-1875*
New York: The Citadel Press, 1950

South Carolina Historical Society. *Shaftesbury Papers*
Charleston, SC: Tempus Publishing Inc. 2000

Shannon, Albert C. *The Medieval Inquisition*
Collegeville, MN: The Liturgical Press, 1984

Simonhoff, Harry. *Jewish Notables in America, 1776-1865*
New York: Greenberg Publishers, 1956

Steinsaltz, Adin. *Essential Talmud*
Basic Books, 1976

Sussman, Lance J. *Isaac Leeser and the Protestization of American Judaism*
American Jewish Archives, April 1986

Swift, Donald C. *Religion and the American Experience*
M. E. Sharpe, Inc., 1998

Tarshish, Allen. *The Charleston Organ Case*
Published in "The Jewish Experience in America"
Vol.2, p.281-315 Waltham, MA: American Jewish Historical Society, 1969
Edited by Abraham J. Karp

Taylor, Alan. *American Colonies*
New York: Penguin Putnam, 2001

Tigay, E. Alan. *The Jewish Traveler*
New York: Doubleday and Co., 1987

Waddell, Gene. *An Architectural History of KKBE*
South Carolina Historical Magazine, Jan 1997, Vol.8 No.1

Weir, Robert M. *Colonial South Carolina*
Millwood, NY: Kto Press, 1983

Wiernik, Peter. *History of the Jews in America*
New York: Hermon Pree, 1972

Wiesenthal, Simon. *The Secret Mission of Christopher Columbus*, New York: Christopher Columbus Publishing, 1979

Wilford, John Noble. *The Mysterious History of Columbus*
New York: Alfred Knopf, 1991

Williams, Mary W. *The People and Politics of Latin America*
Ginn & Co., 1955

Wise, Isaac M. *Reminiscences* (Ed. David Philipson)
Cincinnati: Leo M. Wise and Co., 1901

Wolf, Edwin, 2nd. *The History of the Jews of Philadelphia*
Philadelphia: Jewish Publication Society of America, 1975

Wright, Louis B. *The Cultural Life of the American Colonies*
New York: Dover Publications, 2002

Zola, Gary Phillip. *Isaac Harby of Charleston*
University of Alabama Press, 1994

INDEX